THE BEATLES

♫ ♫

THE BEATLES

THE MUSIC WAS NEVER THE SAME

MARVIN MARTIN

AN iMPACT BioGRAPHY ♪♩

Franklin Watts
A Division of Grolier Publishing
New York · London · Hong Kong · Sydney
Danbury, Connecticut

To
MICHAEL, ANDREA, JOSHUA, AND JESSICA
AND
IN MEMORY OF
GLORIA

Interior Design by Molly Heron

Insert #1 photographs ©: Hulton Deutsch Collection: 1 top; Popperfoto: 1 bottom; Globe Photos: 2 (Tom Hanley/Camera Press); Retna Ltd: 3 (David Redfern); Star File, Inc.: 4 (Jurgen Vollmer); Archive Photos: 5; Globe Photos: 6; Archive Photos/Frank Driggs Collection: 7 bottom; UPI/Bettmann: 7 top; Hulton Deutsch Collection: 8; London Features International Ltd.: 9; Star File, Inc.: 10 top (Jurgen Vollmer/K & K); Archive Photos/Popperfoto: 10 bottom; 11 (Astrid Kirchherr/K & K), 12 (Max Scheler/K & K); Rex Features London: 13; Archive Photos/Popperfoto: 14, 15; Apple Corps. Ltd.: 16.

Insert #2 photographs ©: Globe Photos: 1; UPI/Corbis-Bettmann: 2 top, 2 bottom; FPG International: 3 (Sheldon Brody); Archive Photos/Popperfoto: 4; Archive Photos: 5; FPG International: 6; Archive Photos: 7; UPI/Bettmann: 8; UPI/Corbis-Bettmann: 9; Rex USA Ltd.: 10; Archive Photos: 11, Archive Photos/Popperfoto: 12; Archive Photos: 13; UPI/Bettmann: 14 top; Retna Ltd.: 14 bottom (Janet Macoska); AP/Wide World Photos: 15 top; Globe Photos: 15 bottom, 16.

Library of Congress Cataloging-in-Publication Data
Martin, Marvin.
     The Beatles: the music was never the same / Marvin Martin.
       p. cm. — (An Impact biography)
     Includes bibliographical references and index.
     Summary: A biography of the four boys from Liverpool who, after achieving phenomenal success as the Beatles, were pressured by international fame and broke up in 1970
     ISBN 0-531-11307-8 (lib.bdg.)   ISBN 0-531-15820-9 (pbk.)
     1. Beatles—Juvenile literature. 2. Rock musicians—England—Biography—Juvenile literature. [1. Beatles. 2. Musicians. 3. Rock music.] I. Title
     ML3930.B39M37 1996
     782.42166'092'2—dc20
     [B]   96-13932
                                             CIP
                                         AC MN

119-1844

CONTENTS

ACKNOWLEDGMENTS

Help! I Need Somebody. Help!

—from "Help!" by Lennon-McCartney

It is kind of amazing to observe the number of people who respond to a cry for help, especially when it is not even a life and death situation. In addition to the normal humane reasons, I have to believe that the willingness of many who assisted me arose from their sheer love of the subject. Following are some of my accomplices in this project.

Starting sort of at the beginning, this whole thing got off the ground with my trip to Bowling Green University in Ohio, site of the Center for Studies in Popular Culture. There, Bill Schurk, sound recording archivist, and his able staff helped guide me through their enormous collection of Beatles materials. Thanks, too, to Michael McHugh at the center for his knowledgeable insights on Beatles lore and for directing me to other sources. One of these was Bill King, publisher and editor of *Beatlefan*, who provided a comprehensive overview and analysis of the past and current Beatles scene. Another was May Pang, former personal assistant to John and Yoko and companion to John during their separation. Her insights, particularly about John and Yoko, were invaluable.

Among the other helpers I should highlight are Charles F. Rosenay!!!, president of Good Day Sunshine: The Beatles Fan Club; Charles McGovern, Community Life Curator, the Smithsonian Museum of American History; Jory Gracen, photographer and lifelong Beatles fan; and the Chicago Public Library for its extensive Beatles collection and its magazine and microfilm file that allowed me to go right back into the Beatles era (and let's not forget especially the patience of the librarians of the Lincoln Park Branch); the Museum of Broadcast Communications in Chicago for its rich archive of Beatles television tapes; and Playboy Magazine and WNPR for making their Beatles-related interviews easily accessible.

A special mention for my son-in-law Charlton Burch, whose remarkable depth in popular culture I was able to tap; for Jeannine Deubel for the use of her extensive vintage Beatles record library; for my support group at the Encyclopedia Britannica editorial department and library; and for Eric Steele for his technical know-how. My most heartfelt thanks as well to Anne O'Connor whose support sustained me throughout.

Finally, thanks for "a little help from my friends," the Beatles.

To you all, my everlasting gratitude.

Marvin Martin

iNTRODUCTiON

After the Beatles arrived, music was never the same. The four young musicians from Liverpool, England, who formed this band began a musical and social revolution in the 1960s, the reverberations of which are still being felt today. In the 1990s, more than two decades after they had become the four most famous people in the world, their recordings are still among the most bought and played in popular music.

Perhaps their impact on musical history is best expressed by a songwriter whose life and career were profoundly changed by the Beatles. Diane Lampert cocomposed "Nothin' Shakin' " in 1958, and it was one of the tracks on the Beatles' 1994 album, *Live at the BBC*, a collection excerpted from their early 1960s radio performances. Although being represented on the album was indeed gratifying to Lampert, it did little to redress the devastation the Beatles' arrival had caused in her career. Interviewed on Washington, D.C., radio station WNPR's *Weekend Edition*, December 3, 1994, she remarked: "Well the Beatles came . . . and that was the end of . . . me and life as I knew it as a songwriter. They changed the whole scene. They changed everything that happened to music. It was never the same."[1]

Lampert wrote her songs in the musical tradition of the 1930s, '40s, and '50s, when Tin Pan Alley in New York City was the virtual cradle of all of the hit popular music produced. "But that music is all gone," she lamented. "The Beatles wiped it out."

She was right. Tin Pan Alley songwriters were annihilated by the Beatles because that group changed the way in which popular music was produced. The foursome responsible for this monumental transformation was composed of John Lennon, Paul McCartney, George Harrison, and Ringo Starr. There were other earlier members, but this was the quartet that the world would come to know as the Beatles.

In the late 1950s, when the group was in its early formative state, it was very much like the many other small groups playing around Liverpool. Mostly they echoed similar brands of American-inspired rock 'n' roll, rhythm and blues, folk, and country and western. The Beatles may have been better than most musically, but their repertoire consisted largely of music that others, mostly Americans, had popularized.

By the early 1960s, however, the Beatles had exhibited some innovative qualities that set them apart. One of these was their ability to produce and play their own music—a music that was new and fresh and set the style that would distinguish them through the decade. Soon after their first record releases, other rock groups were imitating them, and record producers were scrambling to find their own version of the Beatles.

Underscoring their watershed effect, *The Ultimate Encyclopedia of Rock* states, "The Beatles were, quite simply, phenomenal. They changed lives; they changed pop music; they changed the world. In writing their own hits, they set a pattern that would liberate popular music from its Tin Pan Alley roots and pave the way for even greater self-expression from the generations that followed."[2] The band's significance is further acknowledged in the *Oxford Companion to Popular Music*, which states, "Clearly the most important group in the history of pop music, their influence is incalculable."[3]

John and Paul, in particular, were remarkable composers and arrangers who have been compared with such famous songwriting teams of the past as George and Ira Gershwin, Lerner and Loewe, and Leiber and Stoller. Astoundingly, a London *Times* music critic even called the duo "the greatest songwriters since Beethoven."[4] George and, more rarely, Ringo also contributed to the songwriting. Before their 1970 breakup the group had composed some 300 songs, most of them credited to Lennon-McCartney.[5]

Another trait that distinguished the Beatles from other groups of the period was an overwhelming personal charisma and charm that enraptured their audiences of young men and women—particularly women—beyond anything seen before or since. The indefinable group chemistry that the Beatles generated remains without precedence in musical history. It was a chemistry so powerful that the Beatles, even after the breakup, continue to have an enormous and enthusiastic fan following to this day. Unofficial Beatles fan clubs thrive worldwide. In the United States the Good Day Sunshine Beatles fan club, for instance, boasts some 35,000 members, holds conventions, and publishes a Beatles magazine.[6] Fan magazines, or fanzines, such as *Beatlefan* have healthy subscriber lists three decades after the breakup. Beatlefest conventions are held every year in various cities throughout the United States. The Beatles have even entered cyberspace, where internet users worldwide can join Beatle discussion groups and exchange information about the foursome.[7]

Beatle souvenirs are in constant demand by collectors. The editor of one collectors magazine, *Gold Mine*, has stated that it receives far more Beatles-related inquiries than any other kind.[8] Any piece of Beatles memorabilia can bring astronomical prices. At one Sotheby's of London auction, for instance, a John Lennon necktie went for $1,320, a 1961 letter written by McCartney for $4,150, and a nude self-portrait by Lennon for $15,000. A letter from John to Paul attacking Paul's wife went for $92,000. Even more stunning is the price paid for the first known recording made by John Lennon with his pre-Beatles group, the Quarry Men, which was auctioned in 1994 for a mind-boggling $122,900.[9]

A third characteristic that distinguished the Beatles from other rock groups, and perhaps the one most responsible for their longevity, was the group's ability to experiment, evolve, and grow musically. As their success and popularity grew to staggering proportions, they were able to strike out into new and uncharted waters of rock, with little concern that they would lose any of their devoted fandom. By the early 1960s, they were playing and recording their own music almost exclusively. The music of 1964, however, was not the same as the music of 1963, nor was the music of 1965 the same as that of 1964, and so on until 1970 and the breakup.

Over a relatively short span of time the style of the music changed, the themes changed, the instruments changed. The musical structure of the early foursome, like most of the Liverpool groups, included drums and lead, rhythm, and bass guitars, with John occasionally coming in on harmonica. But before it was all over an Indian sitar (George) could be heard on some records, a piano (usually Paul) on others, electronic effects on some, and even a full symphony orchestra on *Sgt. Pepper's Lonely Hearts Club Band*.

The songs of their early fame concentrated heavily on the joys and afflictions of teenage love. But in their "mature" years, from about 1965 to 1970, the Beatles gave expression to their hearts, their age, and their generation. That their message was not just of the moment, however, is evidenced by their unremitting influence generations later.

Hardly a rock band is playing today that cannot identify in some way with what the Beatles were doing in the '60s.

There is no standard against which the Beatles' popularity can be measured. There have been other entertainers who were idolized by fanatical followings—Frank Sinatra, Elvis Presley, and numerous rock groups, such as the Rolling Stones, the Grateful Dead, and Nirvana. But none can compare with the Beatles. They set their own standard of popularity worldwide.

The ultimate product of the Beatles' popularity, and clearly a segment of any social history of the 1960s, was Beatlemania: the wild adulation of their fans and scenes of utter pandemonium that characterized their appearances at concerts or anywhere else. The picture of surging mobs of young fans, mostly teenage girls, desperately trying to break through police lines to get near or touch a Beatle, of girls weeping and fainting in a kind of hysterical ecstasy, and of policemen carrying away their limp bodies were common to their every appearance. Their concerts were always the toughest ticket in town; it was reported that even Frank Sinatra and Dean Martin could not get tickets for the Beatles' 1964 Hollywood Bowl show.[10] Young fans went to any means necessary to obtain tickets, even if it meant spending a whole year's allowance. And this was just to see them perform; *hearing* them was next to impossible at a live concert because the din of shouting and screaming that mounted from the moment they stepped on stage generally drowned out their music. It mostly didn't matter to their worshiping fans, who were satisfied just to be in the presence of their idols.

The Beatles constantly had to be smuggled in and out of concert halls and hotels in disguises, exiting through back doors and into waiting vehicles. Once they were even wrapped in blankets and carried out on stretchers to a waiting ambulance. Security was intense. Without appropriate precautions the fab four were in danger of having their clothes ripped from their bodies, of their hair being clipped or torn off, and even of physical injury from their well-meaning but overzealous admirers. The Beatles' first movie, *A Hard Day's Night* (1964), documents the means to which the group went to escape the frenzied pursuit of adoring fans.

Their talent, charisma, and popularity combined to make the Beatles the most financially successful singing group of the sixties, if not of all time. In live concerts they set record after record in attendance and box-office receipts. Similarly, many of the records they set in the recording industry still stand today.

When the Beatles came to the United States for their first tour in 1964, their appearance on the *Ed Sullivan Show* drew a record audience of more than 73.5 million, at that time the largest ever to view an entertainment program.[11] That same year on the Beatles' second U.S. tour, Charles O. Finley, then owner of the Kansas City A's baseball team, persuaded the Beatles to play an unscheduled concert in the city for what was then the staggering fee of $150,000: it was the largest amount that had ever been paid for a single performance in the United States.[12]

On their third visit to the United States, in 1965, the Beatles opened their tour at Shea Stadium in New York City, where they drew 55,600 fans and box-office receipts of $304,000, both of which broke records for a one-night performance.[13]

The number of albums the Beatles sold is, if anything, even more spectacular than their concert attendance records. The Beatles name on any item virtually assures its marketability, but their name on a record label is sheer gold, to the delight of such record companies as EMI and Apple Corps in Britain and Capitol Records in the United States, holders of the distribution rights to Beatles' recordings. In a 1968 statement EMI reported that from the time of the Beatles' first British recording in 1962 to the end of 1967, they had already sold the equivalent of 206 million singles.[14] Capitol Records reported in 1964 that "I Want to

Hold Your Hand" had become the fastest-selling single in its history. In fact, that single and the Beatles' first U.S. album sold 1,000,000 and 800,000 discs respectively in the first three weeks after release, making them then the hottest-selling records in American history, according to the Recording Industries Associations of America (R.I.A.A.).[15] Later that year "Can't Buy Me Love" became the first record ever to sell more than a million copies *before* it was released. Capitol, which had long resisted distributing Beatles recordings, reported the highest gross sales in its history for 1964 after finally—the demand having become patently obvious—releasing its first Beatles products.[16]

The 1994 *Guinness Book of World Records* reported that the Beatles are the most successful recording group of all time, having sold more than one billion discs and tapes. And of course they have sold many millions more as individual performers. Other records for the group listed by that publication include: most multiplatinum (sales of more than 2 million) albums (a total of 11); most number-one singles (20); most number-one albums (15); and the greatest advance sale for a single record (2.1 million for "Can't Buy Me Love," released March 21, 1965).

In addition, John Lennon and Paul McCartney are deemed the most successful songwriters of all time, based on their authorship of number-one singles. They have composition credits, mostly as coauthors but also singly, for thirty-two number-one hits in the United States and twenty in Great Britain.[17]

The Beatles stopped making records as a group in 1970, but the record companies continued to produce retrospective albums through the 1970s, '80s, and '90s—all of which were immediate hits. When *Live at the BBC* was released in 1994 it immediately climbed into the top five and remained on the British and American charts for months thereafter. This feat came years after the breakup and twenty-eight years after their last live concert.[18]

The Beatles became enormously wealthy, of course. So

why did they end it? There's no simple answer, and the theories abound. But there are throngs who argue that it never did end. True, the group broke up, but their presence, their music, their legacy remains. They chose their separate professional paths after 1970, and they continued to be successful, particularly Paul and John (until John's untimely death in 1980). Their individual accomplishments, however, never matched their achievements as a group. As Mark Hertsgaard remarked in the *New Yorker* magazine, "the sum of the four of them was much, much greater than the sum of the individual parts."[19]

The Beatles have had their detractors, especially in the early days, when commentators, such as celebrity reporter Walter Winchell, saw them as a flash in the pan whose popularity would quickly run its course. Today the one thing critics cannot say about the Beatles is that they won't last. For the most part they have outlasted their critics. Not only have their fans kept up the demand for their music, but the twenty-five-year vigil they have held in hopes of a Beatles reunion was finally rewarded. In 1995 the three remaining Beatles returned to the studio to record new material for a multi-part television documentary covering the group's entire history. And they became a foursome again on some of the material, with the remaining three Beatles' voices being dubbed onto recordings that John made before his death.

The Beatles' success going into the turn of the century is no surprise to their fans, even as it astonishes their detractors. Even John Lennon, who was often acknowledged as the group's leader, could not fully envision the staying power of the Beatles in popular music and in society. After the breakup he sang in one of his songs, "the dream is over." Perhaps John really thought it was. But the dream did not end, and quite probably it never will.

PROLOGUE
A MOMENT FROZEN
IN TIME

ew York City, February 7, 1964. Even in New York
City little is stirring at 4:00 A.M., an hour before the
first glints of light will fringe the darkness. Only the
beam of an occasional taxi's headlights or the shout of an
all-night reveler pierces the night. On this morning, however, small, mostly female, shapes can already be seen stirring in the predawn at John F. Kennedy International
Airport. Through the morning hours the crowd swells,
jamming the terminal. By 6:00 A.M. the airport is crammed
with teenagers hoping to catch a glimpse of their four idols,
who at this point are just leaving London on Pan American
Flight 101. The teenaged multitude, transistor radios
pressed to their ears, is ignited by the first progress report
from a local disc jockey: "It is now 6:30 A.M. Beatle time.
They left London 30 minutes ago. They are out over the
Atlantic Ocean, heading for New York. The temperature is
32 Beatle degrees."

Seven hours later the plane lands and the atmosphere
is electric. The Pan Am door swings open, and the Beatles
emerge. Pandemonium. The screams come in an ear-
shattering crescendo stratified from ground level to obser-

vation deck to rooftop, teen bodies dangling over the rail, surging against police lines, crushed buglike against the glass terminal walls, singing, laughing, weeping, fainting, yelling in an explosion of mass ecstasy: "we love you Beatles, we love you."

Yes, the Beatles had arrived in the United States. Beatlemania had arrived. The screaming had started. And it would not stop for three years. Britons had once again invaded the American shore, only this time it was four lads from Liverpool—and they would win.[1]

PENNY LANE AND STRAWBERRY FIELDS

Liverpool has three things which it is famous for—soccer, fighting, comedians.

—Hunter Davies, *The Beatles: The Authorized Biography*

L iverpool grew up as a port city on the northwest coast of England. It was founded in 1207 by King John as a departure point for troops traveling across the Irish Sea to do battle in Ireland. Located on the north shore of the Mersey River estuary, Liverpool lies in a region called Merseyside that spreads over both banks of the estuary. The city experienced prosperity during the 17th century when it became involved in the slave trade, sending manufactured goods to Africa to buy slaves who were exchanged in the West Indies for molasses, sugar, and spices. Industries related to these imports developed in the region. Liverpool continued to be a significant port after the slave trade ceased in 1807, but it declined after World War II, although shipping continued to be important.

Like many seaports, Liverpool developed a reputation as a rough city with some of its poorer neighborhoods especially noted for their young toughs. The city's port also brought great cultural diversity. Trade with Ireland led to a large Irish immigration, and there were substantial communities of Welsh, Chinese, and other ethnic groups, including a black community. The city boasts one of the finest art museums in England, a symphony orchestra, and two soccer teams over which there is much rivalry and civic pride. Atop each tower of the Royal Liver Building is a sculpture of the mythical liver bird, for which the city is said to have been named.

Liverpool has one rather offbeat reputation: it's noted for the number of comedians it has produced, which might seem odd for a heavily industrial city. On the other hand, it is also reputed for the amount of roughneck fighting that goes on there, which is what you might expect of an industrial port city, especially one that has had to struggle with more than its share of poverty, unemployment, and slum neighborhoods. To visitors who ask why the city has produced so many comedians, the locals generally respond humorously with something like, "well, it takes a comedian to live in a place like this." It's not surprising then that the Beatles have been frequently cited for their quick wit and dry, off-the-wall, and sometimes sardonic, senses of humor. In an article in the *New Yorker* magazine, book reviewer Adam Gopnik observed, "The Beatles, for all their depths and their occasional chills, were comedians, with a comedian's attitude toward other people's culture."[1]

Natives of Liverpool are called Liverpudlians, and they speak in a somewhat nasal and distinctive dialect called Scouse, of which the Beatles are outstanding exponents. One characteristic of the dialect is the occasional use of "me," where in English a person would commonly use "my." For example Ringo might talk about playing "me drooms" (for drums). Terms like "gear" (great), "barmy" (crazy), and "sarnie" (sandwich) are also common to Liverpudlians.

In Merseyside, and throughout Britain as well, the music scene was exploding by the last half of the 1950s. World War II was almost ten years past, young men were no longer being drafted, jobs were hard to find in a slumping economy, and somehow music became the outlet for a generation of war babies and the first wave of baby

boomers. The boomers were the bumper crop of cl
born after the war as returning servicemen, making
lost time, married and had families all at once. The first of
this population bulge began hitting its teens in the late
1950s and early 1960s.

Ringo Starr, commenting on the effect of the end of the
draft in 1960, stated that "we were the first generation that
didn't get regimented. . . . Music was a way out. . . . Back
then every street had a band. . . . We all picked up guitars
and drums and filled our time with music."[2] Throughout
Britain, youths at loose ends sought an identity. There were
many youth groups in Britain during the unsettled 1950s,
but perhaps none more prominent than the teddy boys,
who consistently attracted media attention with their outrageous antics. They were conspicuous by their dress alone,
which roughly imitated the style popular during the reign
of Edward VIII, from whom they took the nickname
"teddy." They wore long, greased hair swept back into a
"duck butt" with long sideburns ("sidies"), a velvet-collared
jacket, and narrow-legged trousers called "dranies" (for
drainpipes).

The "teds," as they were called, in typical gang fashion
roughed up anyone who crossed them, engaged in gang
wars, and sometimes started riots at dances, in theaters,
and at other public venues. One of their more widely reported rowdyisms was to rip up cinemas during showings
of the Bill Haley film, *Rock Around the Clock*, the title song of
which seemed to drive them into a frenzy. The song was
also used in the movie *Blackboard Jungle* and came to be
identified with the young toughs portrayed in the drama,
who were ostensibly role models for the teds. Their association with early rock probably did as much as anything to
raise resistance to the new music and drive the younger
and older generations in the United Kingdom ever farther
apart.

The teds were followed in the early 1960s by two other
groups, the mods (modernists) and rockers, whose struggle

for dominance often ended in violent clashes. Both mods and rockers were part of the baby-boomer bulge, and both came largely from working- and middle-class families. The mods were distinguished by their more overt disposition to modern fashions of dress, often imitating continental styles. They usually wore their hair shorter than the teds, and many of them favored motor scooters for transportation. The Who was a band favored by the mods, and that group's rock-opera albums, *Tommy* and *Quadrophenia*, which depicted the mod culture, were adapted for stage and screen.

The rockers were more of an extension of the teds. They had the greased-back hair, but they tended to dress in black leather and wear sunglasses, thus resembling, as much as anything, a U.S. motorcycle gang. And, in fact, for many the motorcycle was the vehicle of choice. They preferred the music played by the early Beatles and others that imitated their rockabilly, rhythm and blues, and rock 'n' roll brethren in the United States. The early Beatles did reflect the hair and clothing image of the rockers but not their brawling.

Brawlers they were, the mods and rockers, and they clashed often and violently, sometimes in the hundreds, causing riots that took whole squads of bobbies to quell. Booze and drugs were common to both groups, although the mods were more into taking pills (amphetamines). But music was often a focal point of their lives as it was for the mass of British youth in the late 1950s and early 1960s, gang members or not.

Not only were British youth listening to music, but they were also making music in record numbers. This did not happen because Britain had an abundance of musical talent. Rather it grew out of something called the skiffle craze that swept Britain in the mid-1950s. What made skiffle so popular was that it did not require a whole lot of talent to form a skiffle group. Consisting of four to eight players, skiffle groups were noted for their odd assortment of instruments. Usually they included one or more guitars, drums, and such makeshift items as a tea-chest bass and a washboard. A tea chest was a type of box used to transport tea, which when put together with broom handle and a string, approximated a hand-strummed stand-up bass.

If the washboard (a metallic board used for scrubbing clothes) sounds like something more likely to be found in an American country-folk band, it would not be surprising. The skiffle craze originated from the Lonnie Donegan Skiffle Group's recording of an old American tune "Rock Island Line." The recording brought fame to Lonnie Donegan, and when Britain's restless youth realized that it required little talent to form a skiffle group, there were suddenly thousands of skiffle bands across the country.

In Merseyside, many young people took to skiffle with abandon. The sound of skiffle could be heard everywhere, in backyards, at parties, in coffee houses and meeting halls—anywhere and at any event where a group of people could gather to listen. Most of the skiffle groups played for fun, and if they could pick up a little cash playing at parties, weddings, or other events, then it was an extra kick. Under these circumstances, groups disappeared and new ones formed overnight. After about three years, the skiffle craze began to die out, but some of the skiffle groups survived. These groups had the talent and ambition to learn different forms of music, such as rock 'n' roll, which like much of the skiffle music, was imported from the United States.

Rock 'n' roll caught on and became the dominant music in Merseyside, with Liverpool at its center. Fueled by the great American rock 'n' roll bands whose records were heavily imported, Merseyside became noted as a British center for rock 'n' roll. The number of rock 'n' roll bands grew, and by the early 1960s Merseyside was reputed to have what was perhaps the greatest density of such groups of any community on Earth. Within the region there developed a distinctive form of rock 'n' roll variously called

Mersey beat or the Liverpool sound. The groups themselves came to be called beat groups.

Among the groups that evolved from skiffle to rock 'n' roll was one led by a restless, sixteen-year-old high-school youth who had found skiffle an irresistible alternative to the monotony of the English school boy's life. Smitten by the sounds of such American rock 'n' roll giants as Elvis Presley, Little Richard, Chuck Berry, Bill Haley and his Comets, and Buddy Holly, that lad formed a group, mostly of his high-school buddies, that went through many changes and called itself by different names. Eventually they evolved into a four-man group that soared to the top of the world of rock as no other band has before or after. The lad who organized that skiffle group was John Lennon; the band they became was the Beatles.

iN THE BEGiNNiNG: JoHN

The guitar's all right, John, but you'll never make a living out of it.

—Mimi Smith's admonition to the teenage John Lennon

The year 1940 was a particularly difficult one for Britain. The country was embroiled in World War II against the powerful war machine of Nazi Germany. By the fall of that year, the Luftwaffe, the Nazi air force, was pounding Britain with deadly air raids on an almost daily basis, and Liverpool, a major port, was a strategic target. On October 9 of that year, John Winston Lennon was born in Liverpool at the Oxford Street Maternity Hospital while, it is reported, bombs were exploding about the city. His middle name, possibly inspired by the bombing, was a patriotic gesture in honor of Winston Churchill, then the British prime minister.

John Lennon grew up in a neat, somewhat upscale, respectable, middle-class neighborhood of Liverpool in which residents largely conformed to expected standards of behavior. Then there was John. He did not conform—not then, not ever in his life. He was impetuous as a child and youth, always seeking trouble and finding it, constantly fighting, getting into one scrape after another, annoying his teachers, sassing adults, and taking the leader's role in whatever he did. You might say that John came by his character traits naturally—or genetically, to use the scientific term. His mother and father were impulsive and carefree, prone to eyebrow-raising behavior and impervious to the community's expectations of proper conduct.

John's mother, Julia, was one of five daughters of George and Annie Stanley, all of whom were strong and individualistic. At age fourteen, the outgoing, pretty Julia was strolling through the park one day when she encountered John's father, sixteen-year-old Alfred Lennon, who had been raised most of his life in an orphanage. Alfred made advances and soon the two were dating. Rash, adventurous, and bold, Alfred immediately captivated the young and impressionable Julia. The very traits that attracted Julia, however, also led to the couple being frequently separated. Variously called Alf or Freddy, John's father had the urge to travel, and he was drawn to the sea. The same year that he met Julia he signed up as a ship's steward, or waiter. Although the two continued to date, they were only together between cruises.

The relationship went on that way for about ten years, when one day the headstrong Julia challenged Alf to marry her. Always ready for a new adventure, Alf agreed, and they were married in 1938. The next day Alf shipped out for a three-month cruise. They continued to see each other whenever Alf came into port, and on one of those visits Julia became pregnant with John. After John was born, Alf supported Julia with funds that he provided through his employer's Liverpool office. This arrangement lasted until about a year later, when Alf got into some trouble and was jailed for three months without pay.

From that point on the relationship diminished, and Alf was seldom seen again. Julia went on to date other men, and eventually she met John Dykins, with whom she became seriously involved. Dykins did not meet with family approval anymore than Alf did, and to end the household squabbling Julia left the family home and moved into a tiny flat with Dykins, taking young John with her.

John seemed to fare well enough in this situation, but the oldest of the Stanley sisters, John's Aunt Mimi (real name Mary Elizabeth), who was very fond of him, felt differently, as did the rest of the family. She thought the sparse and cramped living conditions were not adequate for John's upbringing, and she further disapproved of the indiscreet (unmarried) circumstances of Julia and Dykins's cohabitation. Mimi acted to have John placed in her custody, at least until Julia was better able to provide for him. Julia was reluctant to give up the child, but she finally relented. John, then about two years old, went to live with Aunt Mimi and her husband, George Smith, who were otherwise childless. Maybe Julia felt that John would come back to live with her one day, but it never happened.

Mimi, a firm disciplinarian, raised John as though he were her own. Julia lived only a short distance away, but John saw her only occasionally as a child, almost as though she were the aunt. He remembered her fondly but with mixed feelings as someone who was lively and fun to be with, but who had left him to be reared by his aunt. In an interview with *Playboy* magazine, John commented about not having real parents: "I cried a lot about not having them and it was torture," he said, "but it also gave me an awareness early."[1] Julia and John Dykins made a go of it despite the family tongue clucking and had two daughters, John's half sisters Julia and Jacqui. As for his father, Alfred Lennon, John only saw him a few more times during his life.

Childless Mimi had suddenly found herself with a bright, precocious, highly active, and unusually imaginative child on her hands. She was firm but fair and provided John with the nurturing, training, and values that greatly influenced his life. John remembered her with great affection and respect. Uncle George, for his own part, was completely captivated by John to the point where he became his ally in working around Mimi's rules and regulations.

Mimi has said that John did not enjoy toys so much as

a child but was attracted more to reading, writing, and drawing. "He'd read most of the classics by the time he was ten," she was quoted as saying.[2] *Alice in Wonderland* was a favorite, and he is said to have read it over and over until he had memorized some portions of it. He wrote his own stories and created magazines and books, decorating them with his own drawings. Despite John's extremely creative nature and his voracious reading habits, the early days of his family were unsettled, and he grew up rebellious and unruly.

John's formal education began at Dovedale Primary School. The headmaster and teachers thought him very bright, but they recognized quickly that he was different from the rest of the pack.

In the *Playboy* interview, John said, "I was always hip. I was hip in kindergarten. I was different from the others. I was different all my life. . . . I thought I was crazy or an egomaniac for claiming to see things other people didn't see. . . . It was scary as a child, because there was nobody to relate to. Neither my auntie, nor my friends, nor anybody could ever see what I did."[3]

John led his own gang at Dovedale and was constantly getting into fights and scrapes to prove he was top dog. He and his buddies traversed such places as Penny Lane and Strawberry Fields, names that later appeared in John and Paul's songs as reflections of their childhood memories. Among his gang members were two lads who became his closest friends, Pete Shotten and Ivan Vaughan. When John left Dovedale in 1952, he and Pete went to Quarry Bank High School, while Ivan, more academically inclined, went to Liverpool Institute, a highly regarded high school that took the top students. Two years later the institute also became Paul McCartney's school.

At Quarry Bank, John, with Pete as his chief aide, continued his nonconformist role and took every opportunity to disrupt school proceedings. His richly creative mind constantly devised pranks to play, and he delighted in disparaging school activities and traditions. He was frequently disciplined and more than once was caned. His academic standing suffered as well. Starting in the highest stream, the top academic group, he ended up in the lowest stream, made up of the least achieving group. But while he was at Quarry Bank, the skiffle craze came to Liverpool, and he was irresistibly drawn to it. He spurned conventional athletics and academics, but pop music was a magnet for the young John Lennon. He formed a skiffle group called the Quarry Men in March 1957 and even played at a school dance the following summer.

Music was not foreign to John's family. His Irish grandfather, Jack Lennon, made his living as a professional entertainer. Jack Lennon emigrated to the United States to take up a career in vaudeville as a song-and-dance man who accompanied himself on the banjo, and he became one of the founders of the Kentucky Minstrels. Jack's son, Alf, occasionally referred to some singing he did on shipboard, and Julia loved music. It was, in fact Julia, who encouraged John's early musical interest. John's half sister Julia, in her biography of John, says of their mother, "she was always there [at home], singing away to herself in the kitchen much of the time."

John's great-grandfather, William Stanley, was musically inclined, and he taught John's mother—his granddaughter—to play the banjo and piano. She in turn taught John to play his first banjo chords. The first tune he learned correctly all the way through was "That'll Be the Day," a popular Buddy Holly song.[4]

Julia loved rock 'n' roll, which was just catching on in Britain when John was a teenager. His mother had a record player, and at her house John was exposed to the hard-driving, gyrating rock 'n' roll of such giants as Elvis Presley and Buddy Holly, who became two of John's musical idols. Unlike most mothers, Julia encouraged her children to listen to rock 'n' roll, whereas at home Mimi discouraged John from listening to the new music.

Parents often feared the rapidly growing craze because, in addition to the musical frenzy, it brought with it a whole new lifestyle. They saw their children adopt the hair and clothing styles of their musical heroes; suddenly tight blue jeans and T-shirts were all the rage. And with the music also came a rebelliousness and a sexuality that was decidedly not what British parents wanted their offspring to embrace. But for John Lennon—the rebel, the nonconformist—rock 'n' roll was the perfect solution to the school and discipline problems of his life. When he formed his skiffle group, even as Aunt Mimi raised her eyebrows in despair, the headmaster at Quarry Bank was relieved that John was finally pointed in a somewhat positive direction that diverted him from his seeming intent to destroy the school.

John had managed to wheedle a cheap guitar out of Julia, which he played incessantly until it was falling apart. At sixteen he was full into the skiffle craze, booking dates wherever he could, playing just for the fun of it, usually for no pay. Mimi disapproved, of course. If John's grades were suffering before, his new interest in music caused them to plummet. Virtually all of his time was given over to music, the sound of guitar strumming emanating nonstop from his room. Later in life John was fond of quoting Mimi's repeated admonition, "The guitar's all right, John, but you'll never make a living out of it."

Nevertheless, when John rather desperately needed a new guitar, he went to Mimi. When it really counted John could turn on the charm and break through tough Mimi's resistance. After some persistence, she finally relented and took John to a musical instrument store, where he picked out a steel-stringed Spanish-type guitar. Mimi dutifully paid a sum of close to $50 for the instrument.

John's early skiffle groups changed personnel constantly, John's argumentative nature and the demands of leadership not being the least reasons why. His good pal Pete Shotten, who played washboard, was steady, and Ivan

Vaughan sat in occasionally on tea-chest base, alternating with Len Garry, another friend from the institute. A banjo player and drummer usually rounded out the band. The group made it known in the community that they were ready to accept engagements. After a few fits and starts they finally were invited to make their musical debut at the Rosebery Street party celebrating Empire Day. John Lennon made his introduction to show business from the open back of a truck, which served as the party's makeshift stage.

About a month later they played another gig at the Walton Parish church. John, never one to hold back, had already started drinking at the gigs. They didn't always get paid, but drinks were usually free for the musicians. John was a little tipsy even as the band started to play. Suddenly he felt a tinge of embarrassment. There in the audience was Aunt Mimi, who didn't know about John's performances. Mimi, however, could not help but be pleased with what she saw, and while what she heard was not necessarily to her middle-class tastes, she applauded proudly.

After the set, Ivan introduced John to another friend from school who was interested in playing. Even in his woozy state John could see that the friend's expertise on the guitar far surpassed that of the other band members and perhaps even his own. The date was July 6, 1957. It was the first day of an evolution that would change the face of pop music forever. It was the day that John Lennon met Ivan Vaughan's friend, Paul McCartney.[5]

BUDDiNG WiNGS: PAUL

The minute he got the guitar, that was the end. He was lost. . . . He played it on the lavatory, in the bath, everywhere.
—Michael McCartney, quoted by Hunter Davies in
The Beatles: The Authorized Biography

In 1916, James McCartney, at the age of fourteen, went to work full-time for a cotton company in Liverpool. Jim was not content just to work for the company, however. He loved music, and despite being partially deaf he taught himself to play the piano. In 1919, when he was seventeen, he began leading a ragtime band called Jim Mac's Band. He did it in his spare time for kicks and cash. His musical life continued until he started to think seriously about settling down, which for James McCartney didn't happen until 1941. It was in that year, at age thirty-nine, that he married Mary Patricia Mohin, then thirty-one, a local girl and a nurse at the city's Walton Hospital.

Their marriage was blessed on June 18, 1942, with the birth of a son, James Paul McCartney. The McCartney's would have one more child, Paul's brother, Peter Michael McCartney, born a year and a half later. (Mike McCartney became an accomplished entertainer in his own right. He is better known by his stage name, Mike McGear, which he adopted because he wanted to make it on his own rather than because of his brother's famous name.)

Paul lived in several modest middle-class neighborhoods in the Liverpool area while growing up. His family was not in the least well-off, but they were hardworking and made enough to live comfortably. His father worked in a defense plant during the war, and when that gave out he became an inspector for a local corporation, later returning to the cotton exchange. His mother had quit her job as a nurse after Paul was born, but she continued to work in the health field, mostly as a midwife.

Paul and Mike grew up together as quite close pals. "They did everything together," his father was to say, "especially the things they were told not to."[1] Paul was a bit more on the quite side, however, although he was bright and always did well in school. He was a bit of a chubby lad and perhaps not so athletic, and he also found being left-handed was something of a problem. "I did everything from back to front," he once said. "I used to write backwards, for one thing. . . . The masters at school . . . they'd throw swinging fits." And riding a bike was another problem. "I never could learn to ride a bike properly," he was to say, "because I would insist on pedaling backwards." No matter how hard his father tried to teach him, he would pedal backwards, which jammed on the brakes and plunged him head first to the ground.[2]

Paul eventually worked out the frustrations of being left-handed, despite various failed attempts to switch him to right-handedness. His childhood was generally a happy one, with some of his happiest moments coming in the summer when he went to Boy Scout camp. He was bright, so school work never caused any notable difficulty in his life. Paul's first school was Stockton Wood Primary. He and his brother went there until their mother thought it overly crowded and transferred the two to Joseph William. Paul was a good writer, and in 1953 the school awarded him a prize for an essay he wrote from information that he says was obtained entirely from listening to the radio.

In 1956, when Paul was only fourteen, his happy childhood suffered a severe blow that would affect the direction of his life. His mother died. The family had only recently moved to a new home in the pleasant neighborhood of Allerton when Mary McCartney first experienced pains in her breast. By the time her symptoms had been diagnosed as breast cancer, the disease had spread, and her life ended a month later in October. Paul was devastated, as would any fourteen-year-old at the loss of a good and nurturing mother.

Jim McCartney, who had been pretty much in the background when it came to childrearing, suddenly at age fifty-three found himself facing the formidable task of raising two adolescent boys. As if that weren't enough, he faced a severe financial crisis. Mary had always had to work to keep the family budget balanced. Without her income it seemed that the McCartney's were facing lean times indeed. Even young Paul saw the pinch coming. He is reported to have asked upon her death, "What will we do without her money?"[3] Quite possibly, it was the blow of his mother's death that sent Paul reeling off in a new direction, perhaps seeking to fill the void she had left in his life. It was about that time that Paul picked up a guitar, and his life was transformed forever.

Prior to his mother's death, Paul had done well in school. When it came time to take the high-school exams required for students who wished to continue school, he passed with high marks. His scores were good enough to grant him admission to Liverpool Institute, which he entered in the fall of 1953. But after his mother's death, his interest in school waned just as his interest in the guitar and music began to possess him. Of all the Beatles, he had the strongest musical lineage directly from a parent. Jim McCartney had had no formal training as a musician, but he picked up the piano well enough to play professionally. After his performing days ended he continued to play at home for his own amusement. Paul followed in his father's footsteps, learning to play and sing with virtually no formal training.

Paul had a bit of voice training when he was quite young, singing in the church choir. When he was a little older, he inherited an old trumpet, which he found more interesting than the choir. Like his dad, he learned to play the instrument on his own, not expertly, but well enough to play some tunes. The guitar really intrigued him, though. His interest in pop music had begun to pick up about the time he entered the institute, and he was swept away by the likes of Lonnie Donegan and his Skiffle Group and, especially, Elvis Presley. He begged his father for a guitar, and Jim, being fairly soft and likely fascinated by his son's sudden interest in music, broke down and bought Paul a cheap guitar for a few pounds, which was the best he could afford.

Paul was hugely disappointed by his first attempts at the guitar until he realized that he was playing a right-handed instrument left-handed. After the guitar was altered to suit him he picked it up quickly and was soon credibly imitating Little Richard and Elvis, who had been dubbed the King of Rock 'n' Roll. Shortly thereafter, the Everly Brothers became a significant influence, with their somewhat more sophisticated musical style. Presley, however, had the greatest impact on Paul, who not only copied the King musically but imitated his sexually explicit hip movements, as well as his hair style and clothing fashions. As good as he did Elvis, Paul's impersonation of Little Richard was reportedly even more smashing. Paul was just one of many British skiffle/rock guitarists reflecting the influence of Elvis, Little Richard, Buddy Holly, and other great rock 'n' rollers of the period. The young musician practiced his guitar skills with a school chum named Ian James, who also had the music bug. The two jammed together, teaching each other and playing together wherever they could.

At Liverpool Institute, Paul met another friend named Ivan Vaughan. Ivan had taken up with a skiffle group, playing tea-chest bass, and knowing of Paul's talent invited him to come and hear the group. Ivan had already introduced another institute lad, Len Garry, to the group to play drums and alternate on bass. The group was called the Quarry Men, so-named for Quarry Bank High School, where its leader and some of the other members went to school. It was essentially a skiffle group, but they played some rock 'n' roll, too.

On this day, July 6, 1957, the group was playing a gig at the St. Peter's Church picnic in Walton near John Lennon's house. Paul was just fifteen, but he was a precocious youth and was as interested in picking up girls at the picnic as he was in listening to the music. After the performance, Paul was introduced to the group. He was advanced in his guitar technique relative to the rest of the Quarry Men, probably including John, and he showed them some new chords and taught them how to tune their guitars. He played some of his best numbers, including "Twenty Flight Rock" and "Be-Bop-a-Lula" and even did his Little Richard imperson-ation.

Even fuzzy as he may have been from beer, John Lennon was impressed with Paul. He could see from the way he played "Twenty Flight Rock," one of John's favorite tunes at the time, that Paul was at least his equal on the guitar, and he knew the right words to songs that John of-ten had to improvise. Paul, in fact, was almost too good.

John agonized over inviting Paul to join the group for fear he would challenge his leadership role, even though he was almost two years younger than the sixteen-year-old John. In *The Beatles: The Authorized Biography*, Hunter Davies quotes John as saying, "I was very impressed by Paul playing 'Twenty Flight Rock.' He could obviously play the guitar. I half thought to myself 'He's good as me.' I'd been kingpin up to then. Now, I thought, if I take him on what will happen? . . . But he was good, so he was worth having. He also looked like Elvis. I dug him."[4]

Once the two came together they clicked almost imme-diately. Paul's living room became the crucible in which their partnership was forged. For hours on end they played together and learned together, the younger musician often teaching the older. Paul first appeared with the Quarry Men at a place called the Broadway Conservative Club shortly after he joined the group. During that evening Paul played John one of his own compositions, "I Lost My Little Girl." John was highly impressed and, always the competitor, was immediately challenged by the young McCartney's songwriting ability. Not to be outdone, John also plunged into songwriting. Soon they were composing together, forming a songwriting team that was to become as productive and successful as any the world has known.[5]

In the meantime, Paul had become friendly with another school chum, who, though a bit younger, was becoming quite proficient on the guitar. The lad was a flashy teddy boy dresser, and he was carried away by the skiffle craze like everyone else. Paul occasionally practiced with the younger musician and was so impressed with his skills that he invited him to hear the Quarry Men and meet John. Shortly thereafter, probably at an early 1958 Quarry Men gig at Wilson Hall, John met Paul's friend, George Harrison. Another link in the four-part chain of musical lightning was about to be forged.

FOUR

AND THEN THERE WERE THREE: GEORGE

I liked music, since I can remember . . . "Hong Kong Blues," that's one of the first songs I can remember (I must have been about four), a real bluesy song. Those were happy times. I went out a lot with my parents. . . . I remember being at one place or another, dancing at the club or at old Mrs. Such and Such. I remember as a baby standing on a little leather stool singing "One Meat Ball."

—George Harrison, from his book *I, Me, Mine*

The quiet Beatle or the serious Beatle are labels that have been applied to George Harrison, probably because the press was always seeking some way to characterize the Beatles. George may not have been as outgoing as John and Paul, but when something needed to be said he could speak eloquently and at length. He certainly did have his serious side also, having been the one to lead the Beatles to Eastern philosophies, but his seriousness was spiced with a zany, understated Liverpudlian humor.

George was born February 25, 1943, almost two and a half years after John. The war was still in full swing and barrage balloons hovered over the city, grimly symbolizing the threat of aerial bombardment. His upbringing was seemingly less trauma-filled than that of the other Beatles, yet when he arrived at early adolescence, the same restlessness and the lure of skiffle music took him over as it did the others.

George's parents were unpretentious, middle-class town dwellers who were content to raise a family without frills or opulence. Harold Harrison, George's father, was a native Liverpudlian who left school and went to work in 1923 when he was only fourteen. In 1926, he went to sea as a ship's steward. During a shore leave in 1929 he met Louise French while strolling on the street in Liverpool. A year later the two were married and their first child, George's sister, Louise, was born the next year. Two more siblings, Harold and Peter, followed before George's arrival.

By the time George entered the scene, his father had left the merchant navy and had become a bus driver. His parents had moved to 12 Arnold Grove when they got married, and that is where George was born. George only lived there until he was about five, but in his autobiography he reminisces about how cold it was: "Cold. It was cold in those times, cold. We had only one fire. Freezing. The worst." Still, he remembers the house fondly: "It was OK that house, very pleasant being little and it was always sunny in summer."[1]

George's family moved to a new neighborhood when he was five, and the nearby school he would go to was Dovedale Primary, the same school that was already being attended by John Lennon. The two boys did not know each other, however, because of their age difference, but it's likely John and Peter Harrison met, being that they were in the same class. Although George is remembered by his parents as a good lad who did well in school and seemed happy, his own recollections of his school days are a bit more sour.

George acknowledges that he did well with academics, but it was not because he liked school. His feelings about school, in fact, were quite grim, even bitter. In his autobiography he comments, "I didn't like school. I think it was awful; the worst time of your life."[2] His good grades were more the result of just being one of those bright kids who was able to coast through classes with a minimum of studying. But he does credit his parents for keeping him on top of his early school work. His main passion back then may well have been sports. He remembers being, "Mad keen on soccer, cricket, swimming, and all sorts of athletics."[3]

When the time came to take the exams for high school in 1954, George scored well, and he was accepted at Liverpool Institute, which took only the brightest kids. George, like John and Paul before him, lost interest in school when the skiffle craze came and the music bug grabbed him, the only difference being that George was barely into his teens when the guitar became his obsession.

Music was not a strong part of George's heritage, but there was some musical inclination in the family. His mother and father enjoyed music and dancing and were good enough to operate a beginners dance class for a number of years. Harold also liked the limelight enough to be a master of ceremonies at social events associated with his bus drivers union. George himself recalls his early childhood attempts at singing ("One Meat Ball"), and his parents remembered that young George did not have to be overly coaxed to perform, and he was particularly eager to put on a puppet show for anyone who would watch.

So it was not all that surprising that when George was thirteen or fourteen, and everyone about him was going bonkers over skiffle, he would approach his "mum" and ask if she would finance his first guitar. It was a used guitar that a school chum owned, and it could be bought for just a few pounds, but for George's family it was a rather large expense. Mrs. Harrison liked to encourage George's musical interest, however, and when she saw his great enthusiasm she gave in with little resistance. It was a fateful moment.

George, who was rapidly falling away from academics, now made the guitar the focal point of his life. He practiced, so his mother would say, until his fingers were bleeding. Lonnie Donegan, who started the whole skiffle craze, was one of George's idols, and perhaps the one most responsible for turning George to music. Elvis, Little Richard, Buddy Holly, and other rock 'n' roll stars also influenced him as they did the other Beatles and virtually every other young British pop musician.

Eventually George realized how limited he was playing a cheap and dilapidated guitar. He knew if he were to really develop into an accomplished guitarist he would need a better instrument than the one he had. So George, again using his persuasive powers, convinced his family to help finance the purchase of a new electric guitar. Now George, only fifteen, could see himself playing in a group, an idea that had been developing in his mind.

As his ideas of musicianship grew, George's feelings about school continued to deteriorate. His rebellion against school was expressed more in the form of his appearance. George hated haircuts and wore his hair long before almost any of his schoolmates. He also liked to wear flashy clothes, including very tight drainpipe pants and, like Elvis, pointed blue suede shoes, much to his schoolmasters' dismay.

In scholarship, George had just about hit bottom by the time he was sixteen. At that age, he took a series of exams that would determine his eligibility to qualify for his certificate and go on in school. According to his autobiography, he failed most of the exams, passing only in art. But this made very little impression on George, who by this time had almost totally rejected the whole educational system.

After leaving the institute without graduating, George needed a job. His only passion was the guitar, but playing brought in little money, so it was necessary, at least for the time being, to find gainful employment. Not caring too much what he did, he sought work through the Youth Employment Centre, which sent him to Blackler's, a department store where there was an opening for a window dresser. As it turned out the window dresser's job was filled, but there was another opening for an apprentice electrician, which George accepted. By then, however, George just lived to play.

After George acquired his second guitar he spent most of his spare time practicing alone and teaching himself from a guitar manual. He played occasionally with other budding musicians, including his brother Peter, who also had a guitar, and his close mate, Arthur Kelly. Another lad he played with was a school chum he had met on the school bus. When the skiffle craze hit, their singular interest in rocking on the guitar drew them together. The two practiced together and learned from each other. The name of his guitar-playing schoolmate was Paul McCartney. Paul, a year older than George, was soon telling George about gigs he was playing with a group called the Quarry Men and a guy by the name of John Lennon.

George's first gig was not with the Quarry Men, however, and it came about quite by accident. He had managed to get an audition at a local legion hall for a skiffle group that really existed mostly in his mind. Nevertheless, he formed a group called the Rebels, consisting of himself, Peter, Arthur Kelly, and at least a couple of others playing tea-chest base and harmonica. Some accounts also include a washboard and brass pot among the band's instruments. When this ragtag group showed up for the audition, they found that the group hired to play that night had not showed up. The Rebels then not only auditioned but played their first professional gig as well. Their repertoire was limited, and they had to repeat the same numbers throughout the evening, but the audience seemed not to mind. George's musical career had taken a giant step forward.

The Rebels career began and ended with that one date, as far as anyone can remember. Through Paul, George was introduced to the Quarry Men and John. The group was playing at a place called Wilson Hall; as usual it was just for fun, or perhaps a small fee. George brought his guitar along just in case, but John was reluctant to listen at first, put off by George's youth; he was only fifteen at the time and John was eighteen. Any doubts were removed, however, when George began to play. John was really impressed, and although he was a little embarrassed to be seen with anyone so young, he invited George to join the group. From that point on, George sat in with the Quarry Men on various dates, drawing closer to John and Paul.

George also began playing with another group called the Les Stewart Quartet. Like the dozens of other groups around Liverpool, they played gigs around Liverpool for kicks or whatever anyone would pay. But George felt a growing kinship with John and Paul. The three boys connected musically in a way that the others did not. It was really George, in a way, who initiated the incubation of the Beatles as a group. It occurred in August 1959 after a schism occurred in the Les Stewart group. The break came just as the band had been booked into the Casbah, a new cellar club that was to become one of the city's hottest jazz and rock spots. Ken Brown, a guitarist in the Les Stewart group, had the contact with the club, and he did not want to cancel what could be a golden opportunity. But he and George could not go it alone. Of course, George had been playing occasional gigs with the Quarry Men, and he knew immediately whom he wanted to invite to play the Casbah date. The Quarry Men, who were in kind of a doldrums at the time, were then reformed with John, Paul, George, and Ken, and became the first group to play the Casbah on a regular basis. Three of the four Beatles were now in place. The fourth was still on his way.

A DiFFERENT DRUMMER: RiNGo

*I never did any drum solos, no. No, never have; never wanted to—
even at the beginning.*

—Interview with Ringo Starr, *Modern Drumming*,
December/January, 1981–82

Like John and Paul, and to some degree, George, Ringo had a difficult childhood. Ringo's mother and biological father were divorced when he was only three. Like John, Ringo has barely any memories of his real father. And as though a broken home were not disruptive enough, Ringo's childhood was further complicated by two long, severe illnesses that left him hopelessly behind in school. The smallest of the Beatles, his physical size may have been affected by these long bouts of illness.

Still another difficulty for young Ringo was coping with his childhood environment. He was raised near the docks in Dingle, one of Liverpool's poorest and toughest neighborhoods. Ringo's rise to fame then is almost a *Rocky* scenario: he fought against tremendous odds to finally become one of the world's four most famous humans.

On July 7, 1940, three days before the Battle of Britain and the bombing of Liverpool was to begin, the future Beatles drummer was born at 9 Madryn Street in Dingle. He was named Richard Starkey for his father, which was traditional for the firstborn son among the working class.

Elsie Gleave, Ringo's mother, met Richard Starkey in

the bakery where they both worked, and they were married in 1936 when she was about twenty-six years old. The couple lived with his family until they moved into the small house on Madryn Street where their son and only child was born. Only three years later Richard Starkey separated from Elsie and little Ritchie, as Ringo was called. The couple was soon divorced, apparently under agreeable terms. Eventually Richard remarried and left the Liverpool area, and Ringo seldom saw his father after that.

Although Mrs. Starkey received a small monthly allowance from her former spouse and worked as a barmaid, she could no longer afford the rent on Madryn. She and Ritchie were forced to move, finding a smaller place at nearby 10 Admiral Grove, where they were just able to scrape by. While his mother worked, young Ritchie was often left in the care of his Starkey grandparents or with neighbors. Despite the struggle of his early family life, Ringo does not think of his childhood as deprived. When asked about his family in a *Playboy* interview, he replied that they were "Just working class. I was brought up with me mother and me grandparents. . . . All the time she [his mother] was working. I never starved. I used to get most things."[1]

At age five, little Ritchie went off to St. Silas Infant's School, which was only a short walk away. He was there only about a year when he developed appendicitis, which is usually cured through simple surgery unless not caught in time. Unfortunately, Ritchie did not get to the hospital soon enough and not only did his appendix burst but a dangerous condition called peritonitis set in. After the surgery, Ritchie went into a coma from which he did not emerge for ten weeks. Then he was recovering nicely when he suffered a setback from falling out of bed, adding more weeks to his hospital stay. By the time Ritchie was ready to go back to school, he had been in the hospital for a whole year and was far behind in his studies. One account quotes him as saying, "I don't think I ever made up the schooling I missed."[2]

Ringo apparently remembers little about his schooling at St. Silas. Undoubtedly, his interest in school waned as a result of his long absence and being far behind his classmates. As a result, he was truant a good deal, sometimes going to the flicks when he could save enough money from his daily allowance for a ticket. Without close parental supervision, Ringo had a lot of freedom during this period, but, although he was no angel, he was not a reputed troublemaker compared, for instance, to John.

Somehow, at age eleven, Ritchie managed to move on to the next level of British schooling, enrolling at Dingle Vale Secondary Modern School. Help in this accomplishment came, at least in part, in the name of Marie Maguire, a neighbor girl and the daughter of a good friend of his mother's. Four years older than Ritchie, she tutored him in his school lessons, receiving a small stipend from Ritchie's mother for her efforts. Ringo credits Marie with teaching him how to read and write, and they were good friends despite her making him tend to his lessons. She remembers him fondly as being "happy and easy-going just like his mother" and was particularly impressed with his "lovely big blue eyes."[3]

Mrs. Starkey started dating Harry Graves, a painter and decorator, when Ringo was eleven years old. After a couple of years, when Ringo was thirteen, Elsie told her son that she was going to marry Graves, unless he had any objection. Ritchie felt flattered that he was asked, but he had already grown fond of Harry and gave the marriage the go-ahead. He found Graves a kind and gentle man, and a warm and loving father-and-son relationship ensued. It was Harry, in fact, who encouraged Ritchie's musical ambitions.

Ritchie had to make up some academic ground to catch up to his class, but he was not hopelessly behind when he started secondary school. No question he could have caught up if he put himself to the task. But any possibility of achieving that end was obliterated when he fell ill again at age thirteen. This time it was his lungs that were affected. He had caught a cold which developed into pleurisy and then into more serious lung complications. Ritchie was hospitalized and out of school for about two years. By the time he returned he was nearly the age at which British children leave school. He was not that unhappy about it, schoolwork not having had much appeal. At fifteen, Ritchie Starkey set out into the world to find a job.

Ringo was a bit limited in what he could do, being on the frail side from his long bouts of illness. After a short stint as a messenger boy, he got a job as a bartender on a ferryboat, but that job only lasted about six weeks, ending after a tiff with his boss. He was more successful at his next job as an apprentice joiner for a manufacturer, Henry Hunt and Sons, although he soon switched to fitter trainee. It was during his tenure at this company that Ritchie's life, at age seventeen, took a serious turn into music.

Although Ringo appears to have not had any great musical inclination as a boy, there apparently was some musical talent in the family. In a 1981 interview with *Modern Drumming*, Ringo stated that his "grandmother and grandfather were very musical and played mandolin and banjo, and we had a piano I used to walk on as a child . . . but never actually learned it." He went on to say, "Then when I was seven, my grandfather bought me a mouth organ which I never got into either." He also did not take to the banjo, which he inherited after his grandparents died. But the drums, he says, "I always felt an affinity with." When he was in the hospital at age thirteen, the staff formed a little band to keep the shut-ins amused, but Ringo would not participate unless he could have the drum.[4]

After Ritchie got out of the hospital two years later, drums became a major interest. When he was sixteen, he put together his own drum kit made up mostly of homemade instruments. "I bought a $3.00 bass drum," he said, "made a pair of sticks out of firewood, and used to pound that. . . . I couldn't really play; I used to just hit it. Then I made a kit out of tin cans with little bits of metal on the snare. Flat tins were the cymbals, and a big biscuit tin . . . was the tom, and a shallow biscuit tin was the snare drum, and so forth."[5]

Ritchie was in his trainee job when the skiffle craze hit, and he, like most of the young folk, was swept away by the new sound. It was about that time that his stepdad bought him a set of used drums for about ten pounds (about thirty dollars). About a month later, Ringo and a few other employees, including a friend named Eddie Miles, formed the Eddie Clayton group, Eddie Miles becoming Eddie Clayton. Ringo claims he still couldn't play at the time, but it didn't matter because this was a skiffle band and a high degree of skill wasn't required. It was musical on-the-job training for all. Ringo, in fact, says that he never practiced at home because of the noise and complaints; he only practiced with the band, and "I made my mistakes on stage, as it were."[6]

Like the Quarry Men, the Eddie Clayton group played mostly for fun, occasionally making a bit of money here and there at dances, parties, weddings, skiffle contests, or wherever people would listen. They also performed for other employees at the company.

While playing with Eddie Clayton, Ringo's drum skills developed and his confidence grew. The first inkling that his drumming could lead to something must have started there, because he was soon auditioning for another band, the Darktown Skiffle Group. That group took him on, to his surprise, and he also began playing gigs with other groups, an indication of his growing popularity as a drummer. His technique was improving all the time, and he had an obvious natural stage presence.

Ritchie followed very much the same pattern as the other Beatles. As he improved and realized he had to upgrade his equipment, he sought help from his family. In

Ritchie's case, it was his grandfather he went to, borrowing fifty pounds to put down on a hundred-pound drum set. He paid him back at the rate of about a pound a week from his apprentice's salary.

The world of music was becoming a stronger and stronger magnet for Ringo. Finally in 1959, with just a year left in his apprenticeship and a fairly secure future ahead, he got an offer he could not refuse. It was about that time that skiffle faded out and rock became the dominant form. Ritchie had begun playing with a group that would later be known as Rory Storm and the Hurricanes, which eventually was heralded as the top group in Merseyside until the Beatles toppled them. The Hurricanes had landed a gig for the season at a resort in Wales called Butlin's. They wanted Ringo as their drummer, and Ringo found himself at a crucial fork in his career path. Would it be life as a journeyman fitter or as a drummer? The decision finally turned on the money factor: he would make sixteen pounds a week at Butlin's against only eight pounds at Hunt and Sons. Despite the admonitions of family and friends, Ritchie Starkey became a full-time drummer. He never looked back.

It was while playing at Butlin's that the name Ritchie Starkey evolved into Ringo Starr. Rory Storm, who was originally Alan Caldwell, wanted as much pizzazz as possible in his group, and he wanted a solo feature for the drummer. The boys all agreed to have more colorful names, and Rory and Ritchie tried a few based on Ritchie's penchant for wearing rings, such as Rings Starkey and Rings Starr before settling on Ringo Starr. The name "Ringo" also had associations with American cowboy lore, a particular fascination of Ringo's. The solo act was called Starr Time, and surprisingly, it featured Ringo as a singer, not a drummer. Some of the singing numbers he performed included, "Twist Again," "Hully Gully," "Boys," and "You're Sixteen." But he wouldn't do drum solos, not then, not as a Beatle, not ever.[7]

The Hurricanes with Ringo Starr played thirteen weeks at Butlin's and then played U.S. Air Force bases in France. There is no indication that Ringo had much contact with the Quarry Men up to that point. It is hard to believe, however, that he did not know of them. He may have even run into them now and again, because they played some of the same venues, and both had received publicity in the local press. He positively had made contact by 1960 during a period when both groups were playing in Hamburg, Germany. The Beatles, then sometimes called the Silver Beatles, played some of the same clubs as Rory Storm and the Hurricanes and at one point were alternating on the same bandstand with them. Members of the two groups, including Ringo, John, Paul, and George even cut a demonstration record (demo) together.

Ringo played mostly with the Hurricanes from 1959 until the summer of 1962. During that time, Rory Storm's group, with Ringo as an integral member, was in great demand. They played the top rock 'n' roll clubs in Hamburg and in Liverpool, including the Grosvenor Ballroom, the Casanova Club, and the Cavern Club, the latter now famous because of the Beatles' frequent appearances there.

In the meantime, Ringo was growing more and more popular. He even left the Hurricanes for one period in early 1962 when they were in Liverpool to go back to Hamburg and play with a group backing Tony Sheridan, a popular British rock star. They had offered Ringo thirty pounds a week, his own apartment, and the use of a car to lure him to the Top Ten Club, one of the city's most popular nightspots. He was supposed to stay for a year, but by March he left, unable to cope with Tony Sheridan's unpredictability on stage.

Ringo returned to Rory's group, but not for long. In August that year, while playing Butlin's for the third time, the popular Ringo received offers from two other groups. One was King Size Taylor and the Dominoes; the other was the group that now claimed the undisputed top place among Liverpool's rock bands: the Beatles. Again the decision hinged on money. Ringo is reported to have said that Taylor "offered twenty pounds a week. The Beatles offered twenty-five pounds so I took them."[8] On that fateful five pound differential turned the whole direction of pop music.

THE QUARRY MEN

Well, you make your own dream. That's the Beatles' story isn't it?
—John Lennon, From the *Playboy* interview,
January, 1971

By the time John, Paul, and George were playing together on a regular basis with the Quarry Men, they were all largely disenchanted with school. Although they were not sure that they would make it in a musical career, music was certainly the focal point of their lives in 1958, even if they were just doing it for kicks. John had finished at Quarry Bank High School. Failing his examinations (called O levels), he was not awarded his certificate of education. His future looked quite bleak at that point. A relatively new headmaster at the school was, however, somewhat more progressive than his predecessors and recognized in John something beyond pure troublemaking. Besides his embryonic musical talent, John had shown, when not creating chaos, some definite promise in art.

The trouble was that most of John's art energy was used to draw satirical, cartoonlike drawings of his teachers or anyone else who he felt should be lampooned. John dubbed his output "The Daily Howl," which he snuck around the classroom to the delight of his snickering school chums. His work sometimes bordered on the surreal.

Good examples of the style and character of John's art can be found in his book *In His Own Write*, which includes some of his early drawings and writings. The work is replete with strange-looking otherworldly creatures, deformed people, and dogs. John seemed to have a fixation on deformities, unusual physical characteristics, and dogs. He also seemed to delight in twisting the language in a kind of wordplay to create unusual imagery. At one point in the book, in the introduction to a dialogue, he writes, "A dog is quietly gnawing at a pygmy under the giant desk. The time is half past three on the old grandbladder clock by the windy."[1]

John's humor in his writing and his drawing is sometimes said to have a cruel twist. Many Lennon scholars would dispute this, however. In a 1967 letter to a Quarry Bank student, for instance, John said, "All my writing has always been for laughs or fun or whatever you call it. I do it for that first. Whatever people make of it afterward is valid, but it doesn't necessarily have to correspond to my thoughts about it. OK?"[2] Even the teachers are said to have chuckled over the way John portrayed them.

The headmaster at Quarry Bank recommended John to the principal of the Liverpool College of Art, which would occasionally make an exception and grant admission to a student who had failed to gain his or her certificate of education, equivalent to a high school diploma. John was accepted into the art college and began classes there in the fall of 1957. Coincidentally, and perhaps fortuitously, the art college adjoined the Liverpool Institute, where John's musical chums, Paul McCartney and George Harrison, were enrolled, as well as his old buddy Ivan Vaughan. This geographical arrangement made possible lunchtime rehearsals and occasional performances for munching students.

At the art college, where John remained until 1960, he met a number of people who were influential in his life. One was Stuart Sutcliffe, who later (perhaps regrettably because he was virtually without musical talent) became one of the early Beatles. Stuart was, however, gifted in art well beyond John or, for that matter, most of the students at the college. John dated a number of girls who attended the art college, including Thelma Pickles and Cynthia Powell, the latter becoming his first wife. Another student John met was Bill Harry, who eventually published the *Mersey Beat*, a newspaper that covered the Liverpool music scene and helped launch the Beatles. Harry also authored several books about the group. The Quarry Men had been formed in March 1957 when John was still at Quarry Bank. The name of the skiffle group, also briefly called the Black Jacks, was not representative of its members because several hailed from other schools. Although the group's personnel evolved rather quickly, one of its earlier lineups included, from Quarry Bank, John Lennon, guitar and vocals; Pete Shotton, washboard; Eric Griffiths, guitar; Rod Davis, banjo; and Colin Hanton, drums. Duties on tea-chest bass were split, mostly between Ivan Vaughan and Len Garry from Liverpool Institute and Nigel Whalley from Bluecoat Grammar School.

It should be noted that the Beatles never seemed to be able to hang on to a drummer. Hanton, for instance, after a failed Quarry Men audition, got into a quarrel while the band was driving in a borrowed van and angrily demanded to be let off in midroute. He was deposited on the roadside, drums and all, never to return to the group.

The Quarry Men played the local scene—parties, skiffle contests, church and school dances, coffee houses, youth clubs, workers' social clubs—and they played for events held at such venues as Wilson Hall and the Finch Lane Bus Depot. During these early formative years in 1957 and 1958, they played mostly skiffle and some country western, but, at John's insistence, they also included a growing repertoire of rock 'n' roll.

Some of the other Quarry Men opposed playing rock 'n' roll but to no avail. The band played many of the current skiffle hits, including "Railroad Bill," "Freight Train," "Midnight Special," and "Rock Island Line." Their rock 'n' roll numbers especially reflected the powerful influence of Elvis Presley, including such blockbuster hits as "Hound Dog," "Blue Suede Shoes," "All Shook Up," and "Jailhouse Rock." The Quarry Men also belted out such rock numbers as "Be-Bop-A-Lula," "Lawdy Miss Clawdy," "Roll Over Beethoven," and "Twenty Flight Rock."[3]

Nigel Whalley played an important role in obtaining bookings for the early Quarry Men. Bright and aggressive, he eventually gave up the tea-chest bass, having been threatened by some tough teddy boys after a gig, and became the unofficial band manager. He advertised the Quarry Men's wares and booked some key dates for the group, including their first gig at the Cavern Club. On June 9, 1957, the Quarry Men joined practically every other skiffle group in Liverpool in auditioning for a talent show conducted by Carroll Levis, Mr. Star-Maker, who held these contests throughout Britain in search of fresh, and cheap, talent for his television programs. Held at the Empire Theatre, it may have been the first notable public appearance of the fledgling Quarry Men. It turned out to be a most disappointing moment for the young musicians, who had been brimming with hope and enthusiasm. Still quite raw musically, they were eliminated after their first performance, not even qualifying for the second round.

Only a couple of weeks later, John and his charges were engaged for the Rosebery Street fair, and only about two weeks after that, on July 6, 1957, they played their gig at St. Peter's Church Garden Fete, during which John was introduced to Paul and the course of popular music was changed forever.

After joining the Quarry Men, Paul continued on at Liverpool Institute. Although his academics suffered after his involvement with the Quarry Men, he kept his grades up better than John and George. Paul may have had more academic inclination than the others, but a major motivation was his desire to please his father, who wanted Paul to finish school. Besides, it was Paul's contention that by staying in school he would have more freedom to play music than if he were tied down with a full-time job.

Although John accepted George as a band member, he didn't really want to be social friends with him. George was barely fifteen when he came upon the group through Paul, and John was disdainful of socializing with anyone so young, never mind his skill and talent on the guitar. But George came to idolize John and followed him around worshipfully, despite John's merciless teasing. George often left Liverpool Institute to go to the art college to meet John after class, much to the dismay of the Quarry Men leader, who was more than likely trying to have a moment with Thelma, Cynthia, or another art college girl.

Despite his youth, George was already a relatively accomplished guitar player by the time he joined the Quarry Men. There were other advantages to having George join up, however. It turned out his father could be a source of bookings for the group. Harry Harrison was chairman of the bus drivers social club, and after George joined the group he was influential in hiring them for various club social events.

The boys practiced at each other's homes, usually in the afternoon when their parents were working. They eventually met each other's parents, and to one degree or another each parent thought the other boys were corrupting their own. Mimi was especially contentious about John's musician mates, her family being quite middle class, while the other boys came from working-class families. Mimi's husband—John's uncle George—paid little mind to the situation, however, and was always amicable with John. The other boys' parents encouraged their sons' musical adventures. John's mother welcomed the boys for sessions at her house; fun-loving Julia even joined in at times, playing washboard or beating a cooking pot for percussion.[5]

The group could also practice at Paul's house because

no one was home during the day. Jim McCartney was a musician, a former band leader, and something of an entertainer in his own right, so he had no problem in encouraging Paul's musical pursuits. The only problem was he couldn't for the life of him understand the skiffle and rock music the kids were playing. Here he was, an ex-bandleader, and why wouldn't they take his advice on arranging and tune selection? Why not some really nice tunes like "Stairway to Paradise" or something jumpy like "When the Saints Go Marching In?" The boys just flatly rejected all his decidedly uncool advice.[6]

The Quarry Men could also practice at the Harrison household. Harold and Louise were quite tolerant of the boys coming over, probably assuming that it was a phase they were going through. They were particularly proud of George's making it into Liverpool Institute—their other sons never even having made it into the upper school—and they looked forward to his bright future. They were disappointed, of course, when his schoolwork plummeted, but they still hoped he would find a good job in a trade when he quit school and became an electrician's helper. Still, the Harrisons, particularly George's mother, allowed his musical activity and perhaps even enjoyed the boys coming over and jamming away.

What really turned all the parents off was the way the boys dressed. John's mother, Julia, was the least critical. The boys tried to imitate the style of the teddy boys as much as possible, and while they didn't have long Edwardian coats with velvet collars, a ted trademark, they all did alter their pants to make them as tight as possible, leaving their parents aghast. But the hairdos were usually more like Elvis, whom they also tried to imitate: very long, swept back on the sides with long sideburns ("sidies," they called them), falling over the forehead in front, and greased into place.

Before Paul played his first gig with the Quarry Men, the boys managed a booking, through Nigel Whalley, at a venue that was to become historic in their development: the Cavern Club. Their debut there was rather inauspicious and a bit of a clunker. The club had been open less than a year that night of August 7, 1957, and it was fundamentally a jazz club. Skiffle, which was partly blues based, was played in the off-hours, before or after the main jazz attractions. Rock 'n' roll, however, was scorned by the purist jazz crowd.

The Quarry Men pleased the crowd with their skiffle numbers, but headstrong John chose to include some rock 'n' roll numbers, including two made famous by his idol, Elvis Presley: "Hound Dog" and "Blue Suede Shoes." The owner was irate over this breach of policy, as were some of the audience and even a few of the Quarry Men, such as Rod Davis, who did not favor rock 'n' roll. There was some hooting from the crowd, and needless to say, it was awhile before the group was invited back.

Paul missed that first Cavern engagement because he and his brother, Mike, were away at summer camp. By the time he returned and was able to participate in his first gig with the Quarry Men it was mid-October, 1957. The group had been booked for a dance at the New Clubmoor Hotel, and Paul was designated to play lead guitar. His performance that night was said to be less than sensational, possibly due to opening night jitters. His big moment, a solo on "Guitar Boogie," was reportedly botched. He avoided lead guitar after that, but his work improved steadily through engagements in November at Wilson Hall, the Stanley Abattoir Social Club, and the New Clubmoor Hall, then back to Wilson and New Clubmoor in December and early January 1958. Obviously, even at this stage, although the Quarry Men were being paid next to nothing, they were good enough to get some repeat bookings.[7]

George played his first Quarry Men gig in February 1958, and soon he was playing lead guitar. John had asked George when he first auditioned for the group if he could play as well as Eddie Clayton, a topnotch local guitarist.

George blew all doubts away with his rendition of "Raunchy," which became part of the group's regular repertoire.

Anchored by John, Paul, and George, the Quarry Men were on a bit of a roll. For John, the first half of 1958 was particularly good. Things were going well, socially at least, at the art college. He was making new friends and dating girls from school. The band was improving, and he and Paul were finding time to sequester themselves and write songs. He had to keep his musical activities away from Mimi as much as possible; she would surely go through the ceiling if she found out how much time he was spending with the group and how little in school. But the upside of his home life was that he was drawing closer and closer to Julia. He loved Mimi, of course, but Julia understood John in a way that Mimi could not. Julia was more like John with her unconventional lifestyle, and she encouraged his music and let him use her house for rehearsal. The two were never that far apart in physical distance, and now they were drawing together spiritually.

But tragedy struck the Lennons in July 1958. Julia was leaving Mimi's house after a routine visit when she was struck by a car and killed almost immediately. The driver was a police officer who was said to be drunk, although he was acquitted at the subsequent inquest. John was devastated. Just as his mother was bringing some new meaning into his life, she was taken away. His sister quotes him as saying, "I lost my mother twice. Once as a child of five and then again at seventeen. It made me very, very bitter inside. I had just begun to re-establish a relationship with her when she was killed. We'd caught up on so much in just a few short years. We could communicate. We got on."[8]

If anything, the tragedy reinforced John's rebellious nature and his defiance of authority. But John's musical intensity continued to grow, and his momentum drew the others with him. Their popularity growing, they had been called back to the Cavern Club, and they also played several dates at the Morgue Skiffle Cellar, a club run by Alan Caldwell, who headed a group called the Texans. This group later became Rory Storm and the Hurricanes with Ringo Starr on drums.

By the end of 1958, however, paid bookings were getting scarce, at least partly because the skiffle craze was drying up. The Quarry Men were all but broken up by early 1959. Pete, the washboard player, was not all that musically inclined anyway, and it ended for him one day when, reportedly, the volatile John got angry and broke Pete's washboard over his head, leaving Pete stunned, with the instrument dangling around his neck. The tea-chest bass players—Ivan Vaughan, Len Garry, and Nigel Whalley—all drifted off, at least partly because skiffle was phasing out and neither tea-chest bass nor washboard fit well with rock 'n' roll. But all were John's old school chums, and they remained friends throughout John's life.

The drummer, Colin Hanton, had left in a huff, and the other guitarists, Rod Davis and Eric Griffiths, were gone by mid-1958, the additions of Paul and George having obscured their roles. Now the group was down to three and more or less starting over again, with few prospects. George, for his own part, had begun to play gigs with another group, the Les Stewart Quartet. By summer, he had left school and taken a job as an electrician's helper. Paul continued at Liverpool Institute in 1959 until he graduated. John, the oldest, who turned nineteen in 1959, told Mimi one day that he was leaving home. He had decided to go off and live in an apartment with Stu Sutcliffe and some other art school students.

The flat was said to be a most uninviting place, as one can imagine, occupied by art students bent on living the bohemian life to the hilt, disdaining cleanliness and orderliness. This, of course, horrified Mimi, whose protestations and pleas for John to return fell on deaf ears. John was happy despite the rancid living conditions: he could stay up far into the night talking music and art with Stu, whom

John admired greatly, and he had a place to bring his then girlfriend, Cynthia. Of course he returned regularly to Mimi's to have his laundry done and grab a hot meal.

It was in August 1959 that the three future Beatles were rejoined for good. Small clubs were springing up all over Liverpool to accommodate the many groups in the city and the growing demand to hear live music, especially the Mersey beat music identified with "Livypool." The boom in pop music developed as the postwar baby boomers came of age and expanded the market. The demand grew as the infectious rock 'n' roll, rockabilly, blues, and country-folk music of such American musicians as Elvis Presley, Little Richard, Buddy Holly, and Gene Vincent was picked up and popularized by British groups. This trend had begun with the folksy skiffle group craze, which died out as rock 'n' roll became dominant in the late 1950s. Crowds at musical venues in Liverpool grew even greater with the development of the Mersey beat sound in the early 1960s.

Several of the clubs that opened in response to the burgeoning teenage musical craving played a significant role in the development of the Beatles as a "beat" group. Three in particular should be mentioned: the Cavern Club, the Casbah Coffee Club, and the Jacaranda Coffee Club. Many of these clubs, like the Cavern and the Casbah, were alcoholic-free teenage social clubs that found homes in the basements and cellars of old buildings. The Cavern had been established in 1957, and while the Quarry Men probably played the venue several times through mid-1959, the group had not yet aroused a perceptible following. It was at the Casbah that things really started to perk for the boys.

The Casbah opened August 29, 1959, in the basement of the large, fifteen-room home where Mona and John Best and their two sons, Pete and Rory, lived. It was largely Mona Best's idea to clean out the basement and decorate it as a social club where their sons' many teenage friends could gather. They needed a band to open the club, and one of the teenage helpers suggested the Les Stewart

Quartet, which was playing nearby. The group accepted the date through Ken Brown and George Harrison, and Ken in particular became so involved that he began to spend much of his time helping to decorate the club. This angered Les Stewart, and in an ensuing argument, Ken and George pulled out of the group. Determined to keep the Casbah date, Ken and George sought to form a new group. George went to his old Quarry Men mates, John and Paul, who then were in a sort of musical doldrums, and they agreed to reunite and resurrect the Quarry Men as a four-man group. John and Cynthia even helped decorate the club.

When the Casbah Club opened on that Saturday night in August, the Quarry Men were the resident band, and so they remained for almost every Saturday night through October 10. This stint at the Casbah gave the group their first real foothold in the city, their first real notoriety, the first semblance of a fan following. Some Beatles authorities contend that without the opening of the Casbah, the Beatles might not have ever reformed to become the most popular foursome in musical history.

Everything went smoothly for them until the fateful night of October 10. That night, Ken showed up with a bad cold and excused himself from performing. The other three carried on alone and did well enough, but when it came time to collect the night's wages, Mona Best insisted on giving Ken, who worked the door, his one-quarter share. John, Paul, and George thought this grossly unfair, a fracas ensued, and the group broke up. Ken and Pete Best, who played drums, formed a group that replaced the Quarry Men as the club's resident band. The other three were left unemployed, but they had plans: the Moondogs and the Silver Beatles were about to be born and the musical firmament was about to change.

Moondogs and Silver Beatles

> A man appeared on a flaming pie and said unto them,
> "From this day on you are Beatles with an "A.""
> —from an essay by John Lennon, *Mersey Beat*, July 6, 1961

After John, Paul, and George left the Casbah gig, the group began looking for a new name. After all, Quarry Men no longer made much sense, John being the only one of the remaining group who had ever attended Quarry Bank school. When the group heard that Carroll Levis was returning in mid-October to hold another talent search at Liverpool's Empire Theatre, the boys immediately decided they would enter the contest under a new name. Being out of work gave them additional impetus to compete, and their failure at the same show two years earlier was no deterrent. They entered the competition as Johnny and the Moondogs, a name made up just for this event. It was a time when many of the top groups had a leader name followed by a group name, such as Buddy Holly and the Crickets, Cliff Richard and the Shadows, and Gene Vincent and His Blue Caps.

This time the group made the first cut and went on to the second round of the talent search. Obviously they were much improved over their first showing with Levis, when they were just starting out and quite raw material. At the second round of the contest, held about a week later, the

63

boys succeeded in qualifying for the finals to be held at the Hippodrome Theatre in Manchester on November 18. Winning in Manchester would mean a brief spot on Carroll Levis's television show, a mind-spinning idea for Johnny and the Moondogs.

The boys scraped together enough money and made it to Manchester, where they did well enough to feel they had a shot at winning. But as luck would have it, their chances were cut short. Each group had to reappear at the end of the show, and the one that got the greatest applause would be declared the winner. Unfortunately, the evening ran late, and the boys could not miss the last bus back to Liverpool because they did not have enough money for overnight accommodations. John, Paul, and George had to pack it in and take the long, dreary bus ride back to Liverpool, their hopes for television fame dashed. Johnny and the Moondogs were history.

The boys realized that, while they enjoyed the chemistry of playing as a threesome, it just wasn't enough. Threesomes were not that much in demand, so they needed at least one other member, particularly one who could play bass guitar or drums. Having both would be even better. Those instruments, they felt, would add depth and variety to their sound and make them more competitive. John found the solution, or so he thought: Stuart Sutcliffe.

John had by this time moved in with Stu, who had another art college roommate, Rod Murray. In his inimitable way of handling things, John offered the job to Stu and Rod separately, without one knowing the other was also offered. Rod, being quite the craftsman, started to build a bass guitar, but a stroke of good fortune allowed Stu to beat him out. One of Stu's paintings in a local exhibition sold for sixty-five pounds, enabling the artist to purchase the required instrument.

Stu couldn't play a lick (neither could Rod for that matter), but never mind, thought John, we'll teach him. John's idea may have been a leftover from the skiffle days, when anyone could join a band. Stu stuck with the group a relatively long time, but he never did learn to play very well and was never much more than window dressing on stage. Not to say that that in itself was not important, a rock 'n' roll group's image being a significant part of their persona. And Stu, with his ever-present sunglasses, had a mystique that added to the group's stage appeal.

The boys at first felt that the addition of the bass guitar in January 1960 solved their problem, even considering Stu's quite modest talents. But it became apparent in due course that a drummer was the key to their future. The groups that were making it all had drummers, and the Mersey beat sound that was sweeping the Liverpool area was quite enhanced by the drum backing.

The series of events that led to the group's first drummer of consequence begins at a place called the Jacaranda Club, one of Liverpool's many coffee houses that attracted their young clientele with live music. The Jacaranda was run by a young, aggressive promoter named Alan Williams. A former plumber, Williams opened the club in 1958 and began booking local skiffle and rock 'n' roll groups for entertainment. By the end of 1959, the boys were not getting much work, and hung out regularly at the Jacaranda, sipping one cup of tea all day and hoping Williams would notice them.

The Jacaranda was in the midst of a bohemian neighborhood punctuated with coffee houses where art students and musicians tended to hang out, so it was a natural spot for the four boys to mingle. Stu, in particular, pestered Williams for a chance to play. Williams let them rehearse there but thought they had not yet arrived musically. He did admire Stu's artwork, however, and commissioned him to paint some murals on the club walls. One group that did play the Jacaranda was Rory Storm and the Hurricanes with none other than Ringo Starr on drums. Storm's group at that time was considered the top rock 'n' roll band in Liverpool.

When Williams arranged an all-star rock 'n' roll concert at a local emporium in May 1960, he did not invite the boys to take part. Williams had big names coming in, including the American sensation Gene Vincent and His Blue Caps, to be on the same bill as topflight local talent, such as Rory Storm's group, Cass and His Cassanovas, and Gerry and the Pacemakers. Vincent was a particular musical role model for the rejected foursome, and his popular "Be-Bop-a-Lula" had become a fixed part of their repertoire. Williams's gala was hugely successful and definitely affirmed his progress as a promoter and talent finder.

Not long after that, however, Williams began to take note of the four scruffy lads who were fixtures at the Jacaranda Club. No, he had not let them take part with other local groups in the rock concert he promoted, but he was starting to hear a kind of polish and professionalism that had been missing before. One firm piece of advice he gave them was: "get a drummer."

In those early months of 1960, bookings had been quite scarce, even with the addition of Stu on bass, and the band was still looking for a name. In April, during the Easter break, John and Paul took off by themselves for a short getaway. Traveling to the south of England to Berkshire, they stayed with Paul's cousin and her husband, who operated a club called the Fox and Hounds. The boys did a little bartending to earn their keep and on a couple of occasions performed in the lounge as a duet called the Nerk Twins. The name was probably an adaptation of a name Paul and his brother used when they entertained the family: the Nurk Twins.[1]

Sometime during the first months of 1960, the boys had adopted a new group name: the Beatals. It was the first of a series of names that culminated in "Beatles." Some sources credit "Beatals" to Stu, but the ultimate name of "Beatles" has been credited to John, who was attempting to spin something off of Buddy Holly and the Crickets, a name that the group admired. In Hunter Davies's biography,

John is quoted as saying that he was "just thinking about what a good name the Crickets would be for an English group. The idea of beetles came into my head. I decided to spell it BEAtles to make it look like a joke."[2] There are a variety of versions of the origin of the Beatle name, but it seems quite likely John could have thought it up considering his extraordinary deftness with words. The "Beat" part of the name, it would appear, was cleverly devised to reflect the Mersey beat music that was now the most popular Liverpool style.

Considering the Beatles' propensity for "putting on" interviewers, it would be difficult to anoint any of the Beatle name genealogies as the one true version. At least partly for the same reason, numerous conflicts appear in the huge body of information about the Beatles. One source sums it up saying, "In conclusion, readers can only be urged to recognize that today there exist many Beatles' stories of varying degrees of accuracy and truth. . . . When next you feel intimidated by an authoritative assertion made by someone with an "I Love Paul" button on their lapel, simply . . . ask the question: 'Says who?' "[3]

The use of Beatals as the group name was very brief. Shortly after Williams's Liverpool Stadium concert, he was contacted by Larry Parnes, a well-known musical entrepreneur who handled nationally known stars. Parnes was seeking musical backing for some of his name talent, and he was impressed with the local Liverpool groups that Williams had showcased at the stadium show. He suggested that Williams invite some of the best Liverpool beat groups to an audition and that he and one of his top acts, Billy Fury, would judge them and pick one to back Fury. There was an extra incentive in this for Fury, he himself being a Liverpudlian. For the group selected it would be a golden opportunity to hit the big time.

It remained for Williams to select the groups he thought would most impress Parnes and Fury. He settled on five bands: Cass and the Cassanovas, Gerry and the

Pacemakers, Derry and the Seniors, Cliff Roberts and the Rockers, and rather amazingly the (then-called) Beatals. Williams had been putting the boys off for a long time, and they had not had many gigs recently, but they were always practicing at the Jacaranda, and Williams must have thought they had improved enough to be worthy of a shot at the audition. It is unlikely that Williams would waste the time of Parnes and Fury listening to a group he felt could not cut it, although it appears doubtful that he thought they could beat out the other better-established bands.

Williams insisted on two things: that they come up with a better name and they find a drummer for the audition. The name and the drummer both apparently came from the same source, namely Brian Cassar, leader of Cass and the Cassanovas. Cassar suggested a local drummer, Tommy Moore, who was a bit on the older side at 36 but was an adequate drummer. He also told the group to change their name, and according to some accounts he suggested they call themselves Long John and the Silver Beetles. John could not bring himself to be called "Long John," but the Silver Beetles stuck, at least for the time being.[4]

The auditions took place May 10, 1960, at Williams's Blue Angel Club, which had not yet opened. Parnes and Billy Fury listened intently as one group after another went through their paces. Finally, it was time for the Silver Beetles, the last group on the agenda, to take the bandstand. There must have been a uniform gulp. They looked about the room in vain for their new drummer, but he was not to be seen. It looked like they would have to perform drummerless when the Cassanovas' drummer agreed to sit in.

The audition began and the boys dressed in black jeans and black shirts with black-and-white shoes put everything into their performance. When they were about half-way through their routine, Tommy Moore showed up with his drums, and they were able to finish with their own drummer. Stu, in what became his style, played with little emotion and often with his back to the audience so they could not observe his abysmal lack of technique. Their repertoire included some Elvis material and lit up the stage with their lively, bouncing style.

Parnes and Fury noted immediately the difference in sound and presentation. This group was different; this group had "something else." When it was over Fury did not hesitate. "This is the group," he is quoted as saying, "the Silver Beetles." Parnes thought they were the ones too but was disturbed by one thing: the bass player, Stu Sutcliffe. He felt that Stu's lack of skill and total disregard for audience contact dragged the other members down. Parnes wanted the Silver Beetles, but without Stu.

Williams, who may have been bewildered by the group's success, put the question to the other Silver Beetles. The boys wanted this gig more than anything, but personal loyalties took precedence; they were a group: take all or nothing. Parnes turned them down.[5] More than likely it was John who was most adamant about keeping Stu with the group, because of their personal friendship and their roommate situation. It was not the only time that Stu's inadequacies caused booking problems, and this became a persistent source of contention within the group.

Billy Fury apparently came away empty from that audition, not willing to settle on any of the other groups. The Silver Beetles were bitterly disappointed, especially after they had come so close as long shots. Their gloom quickly dissipated, however, when they got a gig for a dance at Latham Hall on May 14, possibly their first truly professional date, and played well enough to be asked back for the following week. In the advertisement for May 20, they were called the Silver Beats. Where that name variation came from is questionable, but it represents another transition on the way to "Beatles." The Silver Beats never made that second booking at Latham Hall, but for once, it was because something good happened.

Larry Parnes had rejected the Silver Beetles for his top act, Billy Fury, but he needed a couple of groups to back some of his lesser stars. One of the groups chosen was the Silver Beetles. They would accompany Johnny Gentle, a minor TV and recording star, on a nine-day tour of Scotland. The boys were thrilled—this was the biggest thing that had happened to them in their brief musical careers.

The only problem was that they had been given very short notice. The tour was to begin on May 20, so they had only two days to make all the necessary arrangements, including clearing the tour with their parents and finding some rehearsal time with Johnny Gentle. They all made up excuses detailing why they could leave school or work for almost two weeks—not that John, for one, was even showing up at school very much. Paul may have been the most creative: one account states that he told his father that the school was giving the students two weeks off to rest up for exams. And his father believed him.[6]

The deal was arranged through Allan Williams, who had become unofficially the Beatles' manager and booking agent. The ensemble traveled together, leaving from Liverpool's Lime Street Station with spirits high. The air was sparking with excitement; they were officially professional musicians on tour. Onward to Scotland!

SCOTLAND AND HAMBURG

We played very loud in Hamburg—bang, bang all the time. The Germans loved it.

—John Lennon, quoted in Hunter Davies's *The Beatles*

The Silver Beetles were swept away by the romance of their first road trip. So caught up were they that three of them decided to change their names, a common practice among pop musicians. Larry Parnes, himself, did not hesitate to change the names of his talent to make them sound more attractive—Johnny Gentle and Billy Fury were both made-up names. Paul chose the name Paul Ramon, because of its exotic Latin ring; George renamed himself Carl Harrison after one of his idols, the American rock star Carl Perkins; and Stu took the name Stuart de Staël, derived from the name of a famous Russian-French painter, Nicholas de Staël.

Johnny Gentle was at first a little stunned by the sight of the Silver Beetles. They appeared a bit toward scruffy, and he wondered if Parnes had mistakenly sent him the wrong backing group. Gentle's feelings about the group changed almost immediately when he heard them play and was duly impressed.[1] A professional with considerable stage savvy, he helped the boys improve their appearance, at least getting them to wear nearly matching outfits. They had only about thirty minutes rehearsal time before their first date at the Alloa Town Hall in southern Scotland. The Silver Beetles were not promoted separately but billed collectively as Johnny Gentle and His Group.[2]

In the future, the Beatles would become accustomed to moving at a whirlwind pace on tour but always traveling first class with luxurious accommodations. That first trip to Scotland will, however, probably always be remembered for its sheer lack of amenities.

Their transportation mode in Scotland was a decidedly luxury-deprived van in which they, Johnny Gentle, a driver, and all of their equipment were stuffed. Worse yet, their itinerary was so poorly planned that they were constantly backtracking and spent much more time in the van than was necessary. The hotels, too, were less than first rate. They received eighteen pounds each per week, which was much more than they usually received in Liverpool. However, they also had to pay some of their own expenses, so their net pay was not that impressive. Despite these discomforts, they loved what they were doing.

After their engagement in Alloa, the troupe moved on to the next booking, which was in Inverness in northern Scotland. In fact, all the rest of the dates were in the north. On their way to the next gig in Fraserburgh on May 23, the group had a brush with disaster. Johnny Gentle had taken the wheel for some reason, perhaps to relieve the driver, and ran the van smack into another vehicle. Fortunately, no one was hurt except Tommy Moore, who had some front teeth knocked out and had to be taken to the hospital. When they arrived at the hall and stated what had happened the manager demanded that they produce a drummer. Gentle and Lennon had to return to the hospital and cajole the sedated Tommy Moore until he reluctantly agreed to play the date.

The entourage made four more dates before returning to Liverpool near the end of May. By this time they were exhausted and sniping at each other. John had never liked Tommy Moore as part of the group, and he ridiculed him from beginning to end of the tour. That was not so surprising, but it was surprising when John unleashed his biting sarcasm on his good buddy Stu. Everybody knew Stu could not play, but while John would not take a gig without Stu, on this tour he rode him mercilessly throughout the trip. It was a rough time for all, but the boys endured, learned from it, and returned to Liverpool a bit shaken but with a new veneer of professional confidence.

Back on their home turf, the Silver Beetles hardly skipped a beat before they were playing again, now with the newfound prestige of having been on a tour. Allan Williams booked them into his Jacaranda on off nights, when his regular house band, the Royal Caribbean Steel Band, did not play, and he got them bookings in local ballrooms as well. The ballrooms, the Institute in Neston and the Grosvenor in Liscard, were not a joy to play. Both attracted the rough teds and their birds (slang for "girlfriends"), and as often as not the Silver Beetles music became an accompaniment to a bloody row on the dance floor.

Shortly after their return to Liverpool, Tommy Moore pulled out of the group. John was at least part of the problem, but the big age difference and the need to settle into a less chaotic lifestyle pushed him over the edge. Probably he also resented having to pay for his own orthodontic work after the accident. Now the Silver Beetles were drummerless again and immediately started the search for a replacement. It just seemed like the group was always trying to scratch up a drummer. About that time, early in June, Allan Williams opened a club that featured striptease dancers. He offered the group the job of backing one of the dancers, and while they at first scoffed at the venture, in the end they took it just for the money.

After a week or so they did manage to find another drummer who played perhaps three dates with them and then was drafted into the national service. Would the group never be able to hold onto a drummer? The Silver

Beetles managed to stumble along without one, playing dates at Grosvenor and the Institute as well as the Jacaranda until the end of July.

Despite the drummer problems, the group was getting better press and was sometimes billed above Gerry and the Pacemakers, who were frequently playing the same date. They also had been getting some glowing notices in the local newspapers. One such review called them, "The five strong group, which has been pulling in capacity houses on Merseyside,"[3] an indication of the growing fan strength of the band, which in that review was referred to as "the Beatles." Obviously this was a transitional point in the name, because ads were still usually referring to them as Silver Beetles, with Silver Beatles sometimes creeping in.

The rowdiness at the Grosvenor got so bad that the neighbors petitioned an end to the beat music, which attracted the teds. The Beatles had been playing there steadily for almost two months, and the subsequent temporary closing of the ballroom considerably cut back their number of gigs, so they had to start scratching for jobs again and resumed pestering Allan Williams. A deal for them to tour with another Parnes attraction, Dickie Pride, had fallen through. But something else was brewing, and the boys' eyes got very large. The Royal Caribbean Steel Band had left without notice, no doubt to Williams's chagrin, for a gig in Hamburg, Germany, and they wrote back glowing reports of the scene there.

Williams took note and dispatched himself to Hamburg to see for himself what was going on. He was duly impressed and felt his Liverpool beat groups were better than the German rock groups playing in Hamburg. "I knew my Liverpool bands were better and the people would go wild over them," he was quoted as saying.[4] Williams made contact with a club owner, Bruno Koschmider, in Hamburg, but could not swing a deal on his first trip over, because the tapes he brought of the Beatles and others were damaged en route. He returned dejected, and then was livid when he found out Larry Parnes had reneged on a London area deal with one of his groups, Derry and the Seniors. Fearing his group would cause mayhem with Parnes, Williams quickly took off for London to try to remedy the situation.

A friend of Williams owned a coffee bar called the Two I's in London, and Williams took the Derry group there for an audition. After the group went into its routine, Williams cast his eyes about, and who should be sitting there listening but Bruno Koschmider. The German promoter liked what he heard, and he and Williams soon struck up a deal to import more Liverpool beat groups. The first to go was Derry and the Seniors. Koschmider liked them so much he immediately requested a second group. The Beatles were still drummerless, so they weren't Williams's first choice. But all of the other quality Merseyside groups were either tied up or not interested.

Williams then offered Hamburg to the Beatles, but only if they could stir up a first-rate drummer. The Silver Beatles had been pushing hard for Hamburg, and now they were bursting at the seams. However, they were facing the old drummer nemesis again. Who could they get who would fit with the group?

It was fate, perhaps, that the Grosvenor Ballroom date was canceled that night in early August because the boys then decided to check out the Casbah Club, where once they held forth as resident band. The Blackjacks were still playing there, with Pete Best on drums, and they had developed something of a reputation. It was Saturday night and in musical jargon, the joint was jumpin.' They immediately saw that Pete's drumming had improved immeasurably over the months. It didn't take long for them to figure out that Pete was their guy.

A few days later, Pete auditioned for the job and was immediately accepted, which was probably decided before he showed up. Pete had only recently left school to begin life as a full-time professional drummer. The Blackjacks were on the verge of breaking up, so the offer was very timely for him. Pete Best became the fifth Beatle, and the first drummer ever to become fully integrated into the group.

Pete was good for the Beatles not just because he was a good drummer but also because he enhanced the total stage image of the group. John, Paul, and George played and sang and had the more direct audience contact. They worked together smoothly with an almost magical chemistry. Stu was outside of that musical core, kind of a loner with a certain mystique. Pete, on the other hand, not only provided the driving beat that the group needed, but he also was uncommonly handsome, with an almost surly and solemn kind of James Dean manner. On stage, this combination created a charisma that attracted the girls. Unquestionably, Pete added to the Beatles' steadily snowballing fan following.

Still, before they left for Hamburg, they were only known locally, and at that, they were considerably behind some of the other local groups in fan popularity. Rory Storm and the Hurricanes, with Ringo on drums, were getting better bookings. Musically, the Beatles were improving but were not yet that distinct from the other groups. True, they were playing some of their own music, more so than the others, but the distinctive sound that made the Beatles famous had not yet been forged. Hamburg would change all that.

By 1960, John and Paul were relentless in their songwriting, producing words and music at an incredible clip. Some estimates indicate that by the end of 1960 they had already written between eighty and one hundred songs. They composed as though their musical souls were bonded together. Almost from the beginning they had determined that everything they wrote, irrespective of who contributed what to the song, would be signed Lennon-McCartney.

On August 16, 1960, the group, again a fivesome, set out for Hamburg in Allan Williams's rickety old van. Williams had decided to take them himself to save money and to see they got properly settled. They took a ferry to the mainland, and their overcrowded van arrived in Hamburg the next day. It was then that the Beatles, for now that's what they were calling themselves almost exclusively, caught sight of the Reeperbahn, the Hamburgian district in which they were engaged to play. They had never seen anything like it: a tawdry neon-lit jungle with striptease shows, clubs, and bars lining the streets as far as the eye could see. Prostitutes hawking for customers mingled with the crowds of sightseers, sailors, students, and businessmen seeking thrills. The boys were gape-jawed, bug-eyed, and tingling with excitement.

Although there was nothing like the Reeperbahn in their hometown, Liverpool and Hamburg could be considered sister cities. They are both port towns lying on a major river (the Elbe in Hamburg's case), and both are located at the same degree of northern latitude. Both places had a reputation for roughness, with large elements of aggressive gang toughs always itching for a fight. So it is not surprising that the boys would come to feel reasonably at home in Hamburg.

Their first stop in Hamburg was the Kaiserkeller, one of Koschmider's clubs, where Derry and the Seniors were performing. That group did not welcome the Beatles warmly, regarding them instead as a second-rate outfit that could not match their own talents. Nevertheless the Beatles thought the Kaiserkeller was a pretty neat place and expected they would be happy playing there despite the Derry group's hostility. They were wrong.

Koschmider took them to another club nearby called the Indra Club, a former strip joint. It was tiny and poorly appointed, and it was virtually empty when they looked in. Then they were taken to their living quarters, which were just as depressing. Their small, smelly, unseemly rooms were across the street in a movie house and were located right behind the screen. For washing up they used the cinema's rest rooms. Not an ideal situation.

Playing at the Indra Club was not luxurious, but it was a learning experience. The boys had been used to playing about an hour a night at a gig. That changed in Hamburg. Their contract called for them to play four-and-a-half hours a night on weekdays and six hours on Saturday and Sunday. On any given night they might even play more if the crowd was demanding or unruly. Some accounts say they performed as much as eight hours a day, and the Beatles themselves often spoke of the long hours they played in Hamburg. The demands of such a schedule forced the group to expand their repertoire, and the noisy and raucous conditions under which they played compelled them to play loud, ever increasing the heavy beat and strong rhythms. It was this evolution of style in Hamburg that forged the Beatles' sound.

Koschmider caused another change in the way the Beatles performed. He had hoped they would bring the dreary Indra Club to life. They started out using the repertoire that went over best in Liverpool. It was good musically, but not as rollicking as Koschmider expected, and there was little audience reaction. He scolded the boys to *mach schau*, or "make show," a common German expression meaning to really let go and be spectacular or even outrageous. Obviously, you don't have to tell a repressed extrovert like John Lennon twice to *mach schau*. Or, for that matter, Paul, who loved to perform for the live audience.

After Koschmider's admonition, John, especially, Paul, somewhat, and George, to a lesser degree, became highly animated on stage. John did his best Gene Vincent imitation, rocking all over the stage singing "Be-Bop-A-Lula," and the other boys performed similar antics. Even Stu let go now and then, romping about the stage. Pete was more confined behind the drums, and he was to say, "There wasn't much I could do from behind the drums, other than stand up or hop around with a tom-tom under my arm."

They "made show" like a bunch of wild maniacs, belting out the hard-core American rock 'n' roll of Little

Richard, Fats Domino, Carl Perkins, and Elvis Presley. They stretched out their best numbers, such as "Roll Over Beethoven" and "Long Tall Sally," to twenty minutes or so apiece to fill their vast onstage time. They played for hours into early morning until they were dripping and near exhaustion. And the Germans loved it.[5]

The Beatles filled up the Indra Club. In their first six weeks, they built up a fan following burgeoning with enthusiasm. They did everything on stage they could think of, including insulting the audience. That was John's specialty of course. He would goose-step around the stage doing the Nazi salute, calling the audience Nazi *schwein* (pigs) and worse, and asking, "where are your tanks?" At times he came on stage wearing only his underwear, and once, on another visit to Hamburg, he came out wearing a toilet seat around his neck. The fans just screamed for more. Most of them couldn't understand John's insults, and those that did were students who were more liberal and thought it was a great show.

The Indra Club was rocking, and Koschmider loved it. Unfortunately, the neighbors did not. There were some residents close by, and while they could tolerate the relatively quiet accompaniment of the striptease, the late-night amplified rock music, and the pounding, howling, and screaming that went with it, were more than they could bear. The authorities were notified, and the Indra Club was closed.

That incident actually turned out to be good for the Beatles. By the time the Indra closed, their contract was nearly up, but it had a two-month extension clause. Koschmider wanted to hang on to the Beatles, and he offered them a gig at the Kaiserkeller. Derry and the Seniors were leaving about that time and were being replaced by none other than Rory Storm and the Hurricanes, with Ringo Starr on drums. The Beatles would split the playing time with Rory, who, naturally, would receive top billing. It was there at the Kaiserkeller that the boys really got to know Ringo, beginning a relationship that would create the Fab Four.

Another relationship began at the Kaiserkeller that would also change the chemistry of the group. There, the Beatles met two people who would play a significant part in their lives: Klaus Voorman and Astrid Kirchherr. They were members of the Hamburg art colony, and were sweethearts at the time the Beatles came to the city. Klaus was a graphic designer and Astrid a photographer's assistant. One night in early October, the two quarreled, and Klaus ended up wandering about the Reeperbahn. Although not a rock fan, he was intrigued by the sounds he heard emerging from the Kaiserkeller.

Out of curiosity he went inside, where Rory Storm was finishing up his set. He enjoyed Rory, but the next group absolutely fascinated him. So taken was he by their powerful rock music and wild *mach schau* that he later implored Astrid to come with him to see the Beatles. She was reluctant at first even to go near the debauched district but eventually relented. Astrid too was smitten, and the couple struck up an acquaintance with the Beatles. They brought their friends, and soon there was a horde of art students cheering for the group.

Astrid was intrigued by the boys' stage appearance. They cavorted about, usually dressed all in black, mostly leather, with pointy cowboy boots, greased hair, long and swept back on the sides into a duck butt, and with huge, high pompadours on top. She quickly saw them as a photographic subject, and Klaus, who had designed record covers, plugged for some day doing a cover for them (he actually did some years later: *Rubber Soul*). It wasn't long before Astrid began inviting the boys home for food and drink and eventually began taking their pictures, many of which are still seen today in works about the Beatles.

Something else happened as well: romance. It is probably not surprising that an attraction grew between the artistically inclined Astrid and the most artistic Beatle, Stu

Sutcliffe. Stu was in; Klaus was out. As their love bloomed, Astrid took photos of the Beatles, some of which are now famous. She was also instrumental in remodeling their image, influencing the famous Beatle hairdo, as well as their clothing styles.

After a couple of months in Hamburg, the Beatles had become extremely popular young musicians, and they were very attractive to the young women who flocked to the club. Unmarried and socially uninhibited, the boys did not often resist the many opportunities for intimate relationships with adoring German girls. Some accounts probably exaggerate this aspect of the Hamburg experience. Even given the seemingly boundless energy of youth, the Beatles spent so much time playing—seven days a week—that they were exhausted much of the time. So exhausted that they started taking "pep" pills to get them through the show. They seldom got a decent night's sleep in their rancid quarters behind the movie screen. They arrived home in the wee hours of the morning, and about the time they came off the pills and got to sleep, the movie matinee started, the sound track blaring in their ears.[6]

Everything was going well for the Beatles in Hamburg musically, though. They even cut their first real record there. Allan Williams arranged it, bringing together three Beatles—John, Paul, and George—and two members of Rory Storm's group, one of whom was Ringo Starr. It was the first time the final four Beatles would play together. The song they recorded was "Summertime," a 78-rpm recording that received little promotion.[7] In their off-hours the Beatles also visited other clubs in the area. One of the clubs they visited regularly was the Top Ten, a rock 'n' roll club operated by Peter Eckhorn, a young German entrepreneur.

The Top Ten had only opened in October 1960, and Eckhorn immediately raided the Kaiserkeller of some of its key personnel, including Elvis-style rock singer Tony Sheridan. This infuriated the short-tempered Koschmider, who took umbrage over his acts being stolen. When he heard the Beatles were hanging out at the rival club and even jamming onstage with Sheridan, he took action. According to their contract, the Beatles could not play for any other club close to the Kaiserkeller for a specified number of weeks. The boys and Koschmider argued, and the club owner threatened the Beatles with everything from bodily harm to deportation. John reportedly told him to "get stuffed."[8]

The first thing Koschmider did was turn in George Harrison for being underage. George was seventeen and the legal age for playing in clubs in Germany was eighteen. Koschmider protected George when it served his purpose but not now. George was deported. The rest of the group had been offered lodging in the Top Ten Club building and were prepared to defect from the Kaiserkeller. They returned to their grubby rooms at the cinema to collect their belongings. The story goes that on leaving, the boys, Pete and Paul specifically, caused some fire damage, giving Koschmider cause to call the authorities.

According to Paul, "we accidentally singed a bit of cord on an old stone wall in the corridor, and he had the police on us. He'd told them we'd tried to burn his place down, so they said 'leave please.' "[9] Pete and Paul were deported the next day. John, dejected without his companions, left a few days later. Stu, who was now thinking seriously about art again, stayed in Hamburg, taking up residence with Astrid. It was December 1960, and the big bang of rock was almost here.

TAKiNG OFF

*On their first appearance I was completely knocked
out by them. They had a pounding, pulsating beat which
I knew would be big box office. When they finished
playing. . . I booked them solidly for several months.*
                              —Brian Kelly, Liverpool Promoter[1]

The four deported Beatles were somewhat dejected upon their return to Liverpool, especially after the high life they had lived in Hamburg and the unseemly circumstances of their leaving. They had crammed some five hundred hours of onstage time into their extended three-and-a-half-month stay and came back much better musicians and showmen but with little monetary reward. Paul, pressured by his father, even sought temporary employment. This lull in their playing career, however, was brief. The boys were highly energized by their experience in Hamburg, and within a few days after John's return, about mid-December 1960, they were raring to go.

Having Pete in the band did not hurt in securing their first post-Hamburg booking at the Casbah, the club being run by Pete's mother. They played a couple of other local gigs, and then one day ran into Bob Wooler, an out-of-work local disc jockey, at the Jacaranda. It was a fateful meeting. The boys asked Wooler if he could secure bookings for them. Wooler had some connections with promoters about town, and he said he would see what he could do.

One of the promoters Wooler knew was Brian Kelly, who was pretty active at that time booking groups into the local dance halls. Kelly was reluctant to try the Beatles, however, because he was the one they had left high and dry when they took off for their Scotland tour. He finally relented after some tough coaxing and hired them for a gig at the Litherland Town Hall, a popular dance spot. Wooler tried to get eight pounds for the boys, but Kelly would only come up with six. The date of the performance was December 27, 1960. It would be a red-letter day in Beatles' history.

When the Beatles took the stage that night, their group included a new member, Chas Newby, who played bass guitar in Stu's place. Newby played only a few gigs with them before returning to school after the Christmas holidays. The Beatles were not all that well known in this suburban area of Liverpool, and they were booked too late to be announced in the advertisements. Kelly did manage to attach some posters about, announcing the appearance of the group "direct from Hamburg." As a result, many of the patrons who showed up that night thought they were a German group and later remarked how well they spoke English.

The town hall was a huge dance emporium that could accommodate some fifteen hundred dancers. That Saturday night there was a large holiday crowd massed on the dance floor when the time came for the Beatles to go on. The patrons had hardly heard of the group and had paid little attention while they were tuning up, assuming they were typical of the bands that played the hall. Most groups at that time were imitating the very popular British group Cliff Richard and the Shadows, a pristinely attired group that played gentle, restrained pop melodies in what one analyst described as an "emotionally vapid ballad style."[2] The crowd that night did not hear another Cliff Richard imitation. On the downbeat, the Beatles ripped into their raucous, Hamburg-enriched rendition of "Long Tall Sally," exploding with a big-beat sound that would soon be heard 'round the world.[3]

When the music started, heads snapped toward the bandstand. The crowd lunged almost in a single, wavelike surge toward the stage and clung there through the set as the Beatles belted out their *mach schau* routine. Their endless hours onstage in Hamburg had taught them how to wow an audience, and they poured it on. The Merseyside crowd had never seen anything like it, and they loved it. They screamed, they jumped, they worked themselves into a frenzy. After December 27, 1960, the Beatles never looked back.[4] Beatlemania was born!

Brian Kelly did not have to be hit over the head. The truth was there before him, and he acted quickly, knowing the demand for the Beatles would escalate from that moment. After their set he immediately dispatched some of the hall's biggest bouncers to the dressing room to ward off any promoters who might try to get to the boys. According to Kelly, he then, "went inside and booked them solidly for months ahead."[5] The Beatles were delighted, signing for eight pounds per show, and happy to get it, but not knowing that with their newfound popularity they could demand much more. Allan Williams was still unofficially their manager, but the boys cut their own deals as often as not.

Through the early months of 1961, the Beatles played regularly at venues throughout Liverpool that had been selected by Kelly. They had all gone back to their homes to live, but none went back to school, although Mimi assumed that John would reenter art college as soon as he came to his senses. John resumed his romance with Cynthia, having stayed in close touch with her through correspondence while in Hamburg. He did not intend to go back to college, especially after Hamburg and Litherland, but to keep peace he indulged Mimi's belief that he would. Paul took some temporary work as a coil winder, pleasing his dad, but he wasn't much good at it and could hardly keep up with it as the bookings increased. He quit after a couple of months. George and Pete were content, for the most part, to hang out in the music scene.

After Litherland, Bob Wooler continued to play a significant role in the Beatles' musical progress. It was Wooler, along with Mona Best, who helped establish the Beatles at the club that became synonymous with their name in the early days: the Cavern Club. Since Litherland, the boys were in considerable demand. They were a foursome now for the most part, with Paul taking over the bass guitar and doing an occasional stint on the piano.

Bob Wooler, who was now compere (master of ceremonies) at the Cavern Club, was the driving force behind influencing the owner into giving the Beatles another shot at the club. In their first attempt at the Cavern, the then Quarry Men had left unceremoniously after their skiffle group had attempted some rock 'n' roll in defiance of the jazz-minded owner. Since that time, the owner, like many others, had softened his stance against rock 'n' roll when it became apparent that jazz could not hold its own against the increasingly popular rock genre.

Now Wooler pressed the club to book the Beatles, and the owner relented in acknowledgment of the group's growing popularity. The Cavern had lunchtime sessions that attracted students and young workers on their lunch breaks, and it was at one of these, on February 21, 1962, that the group made its debut there as the Beatles. There is some debate over the numbers, but from that day until August 1963, the Beatles reportedly played an incredible 292 dates at the Cavern Club.

They continued to play other local spots, including the big, sometimes rough, dance halls, and it became common for them to play two, even three, different gigs on a single day. But the Cavern became home. At first they played the lunchtime sessions, but with the demand from their growing fandom, they were soon playing the evening slots as well.

Eventually, as the Cavern switched over entirely to rock 'n' roll, it became so popular that fans sometimes literally camped outside to assure getting in. According to one fan, the club was "a series of black cellars underneath a dirty, disused warehouse . . . and when we are queuing up for the lunchtime session . . . we have to watch out for the large lorries [trucks] . . . trying to squeeze past each other. . . . For the Beatles we used to sleep outside all night."[6] Hundreds of bodies would jam into that dimly lit, dank underground emporium. One can only assume that the music must have been great because the patrons seemed oblivious to the lack of Cavern Club amenities, including even decent air to breath.

Mark Lewisohn, the Beatles archivist, describes the Cavern Club as a "health inspector's nightmare . . . no ventilation, no dramatic lighting, other than a set of 60-watt white bulbs, starkly pointing down at the stage, dreadfully inadequate lavatory arrangements, no tables . . . and most certainly no room."[7] Once the music started, the amps turned up as high as they would go, the scene became frenzied. A London newspaper feature on the Beatles described an early Cavern Club performance:

> The beat went on for three solid hours. Within minutes perspiration was streaming down the walls and dripping steadily from the ceiling onto the pulsating bodies of several hundred dancers. . . . Late in the night, an exhausted crowd filed up the narrow staircase. The boys stripped off their shirts and wrung them out in the narrow street.[8]

The moisture in the club was no joke; the sweating from the walls and the bodies was so excessive that it occasionally shorted out the band's amplifiers. It was at the Cavern Club that the idolization of the Beatles really took hold, with girls following them, flirting, and making it difficult for them to move about. Beatlemania was building.

It was not just in Liverpool that the Beatles were in demand. Hamburg continued to beckon. Peter Eckhorn remembered the Beatles well and wanted them back for his spacious Top Ten Club, but it was not easy to arrange considering the dubious circumstances of their departure a few months earlier. The authorities had to be appeased, but Eckhorn managed it, and with George now eighteen, nothing stood in their way. On March 24, 1961, they departed for their second stand in Hamburg.

This foray into West Germany was done in high style compared to the first. They traveled more comfortably by train this time, and Eckhorn had accommodations for them above the Top Ten, which although still without the comforts of a decent hotel, had its own bathroom, and it sure beat living behind the screen of a movie theater. The Top Ten, too, was a considerable improvement over the Kaiserkeller as a place to play, drawing a somewhat more sophisticated clientele. Pete Best was mostly responsible for negotiating the contract with Eckhorn, which virtually signaled the end of the boys' business relationship with Allan Williams, who was miffed.

The contract was as outlandishly demanding as before, but for a more livable, if still modest, wage. They were to be paid thirty-five West German marks (about nine dollars) each per day, and they were to work seven days a week, from 7:00 P.M. until 2:00 A.M. Monday through Friday, and until 3:00 A.M. on weekends. The contract was for the month of April.[9] It was a grueling schedule, but again it forced the Beatles to expand their repertoire and to continue to develop rapidly as musicians and as showmen.

Astrid and Stu greeted the other Beatles when they returned to Hamburg. Stu rejoined the group on occasion but never again became a full-time member. Mostly it was John, Paul, George, and Pete playing together and alternating on the bandstand with Tony Sheridan. The Beatles were now heavily experienced and swelling with confidence, and their popularity caught fire in Hamburg as it had in Liverpool. Sheridan was still the headliner in the club, but the Beatles were packing them in as well.

During this visit to Hamburg, the Beatles made the first record on which they were officially recognized. A German recording executive caught their act at the Top Ten and was excited by what he heard. His original intention had been to check out Tony Sheridan as possible recording material, but in the end he also wanted the Beatles, who sometimes worked onstage with Sheridan to back him. The final arrangements were made by Berthold Kaempfert, a composer, arranger, and conductor, and a promoter for the pop-music label Polydor.

In May 1961, the Beatles recorded several songs with Sheridan, including "My Bonnie" and "The Saints" ("When the Saints Go Marching In"), which did well on the West German charts. On the record label they were called the Beat Brothers, because Beatles could be confused for a German slang word. The session also featured the first recording of an original Beatle work, "Cry for a Shadow," an instrumental guitar piece composed by John and George. They were paid a small session fee for their work and received no royalties. Although Sheridan was Kaempfert's primary focus, he liked the Beatles well enough to sign them to a contract that was voided a year later.

The other significant thing that happened to the Beatles during this Hamburg engagement was a fundamental change in their appearance, a first step toward what became the Beatles' image. It was instigated by their friend and Stu's sweetheart, Astrid. She had ideas about style and fashion, and she convinced Stu that he should change his image. She started with his hair. First she washed out all the grease, and then she cut it so that it fell over the ears and across the forehead. It was not a completely original cut for Western Europe, and it was the style adopted by most of Astrid and Klaus's friends. In the future, however, a version of the cut Astrid gave Stu would be called a "Beatle cut."

When Stu first showed up with his new hairstyle, the other band members laughed hysterically and teased Stu mercilessly, something they did a lot of anyway because he was such a lousy musician. But the Beatles really identified more with the art crowd, the "exis" (for existentialist) as John called them, and the boys one by one succumbed to the new style, the strong-headed John being the last except for Pete, who never did adopt the hairstyle. He preferred his greasy Elvis look, and he was most popular with the girls, so why change?[10] That decision by Pete may have been symptomatic of underlying differences between himself and the others that led to future problems.

Astrid also designed a collarless jacket that Stu was the first to wear and was also eventually adopted by the others. That type of jacket became another Beatles trademark in years to come. Mainly, however, in those Hamburg days the boys wore black leather pants and jackets, the latter worn open with a black T-shirt showing beneath, and pointed boots. Astrid herself was fond of wearing black leather.

The boys lived it up in Hamburg as they had done before, but after two extensions of their contract, they were ready to return home. They were probably tired and needed a break from the exhaustive Top Ten routine. In early July, they packed it in and headed back to the familiar surroundings of Liverpool and the comforts of home. Liverpool, and especially the Cavern Club, welcomed them back with open arms.

REINVENTING THE BEATLES: BRIAN EPSTEIN

They were rather scruffy dressed . . . and they had a rather untidy stage appearance.

—Brian Epstein's first impression of the Beatles, from Mark Lewisohn's *The Beatles Live!*

"**W**here are we going, fellas?" "To the top, Johnny!" "What top?" "To the toppermost of the poppermost, Johnny!" It was the battle cry of the Beatles. When things got tough and the boys were getting down and needed a lift, John would shout out the above questions and the other three would respond in unison with the above answers. One such time was mid-1961 after the Beatles returned from their second Hamburg trip. There were plenty of bookings and their local fandom continued to build, but outside of Hamburg and Liverpool they were still unknown. The big-time London music critics would take no note of the Merseyside beat scene at all. The feeling in the band was that they had reached the top in Merseyside, they were too good to stay local, and they needed to find new worlds to conquer. But they were stymied, not knowing how to take the next step nor anyone who could help them. That would soon change.

The Beatles and the local promoters plugged the record the boys had made in Hamburg as much as possible. There was one major problem: there were only a few copies in Liverpool—the ones that belonged to the boys personally.

The fans, of course, hearing that their idols had made a record, wanted copies and sought them out in the local record stores. This is what the Beatles wanted, hoping that the demand would cause some to be imported. No one seemed interested enough to take a chance though; not at least until one day in late October when a fan walked into the record department of the local NEMS department store and asked for a record of "My Bonnie" by Tony Sheridan with the Beat Brothers. The fastidious record department proprietor was stunned when his well-updated and comprehensive files revealed nothing about the record or its artists.

Brian Epstein, the proprietor, did not like defeat; furthermore, he was a bit bored, and he loved the challenge of providing difficult-to-find records for his customers. It was this characteristic that led to one of the most fruitful business relationships in entertainment history. There were other requests for the record, and Epstein was determined to track it down. He found out quickly, of course, that the demand for the record was stirred not by Tony Sheridan, but by the Beatles, alias the Beat Brothers, who accompanied Sheridan.

The curious thing is that Epstein later claimed that he had never heard of the Beatles at the time of the requests. That would seem improbable for several reasons, the primary one being that he wrote a column for *Mersey Beat*, a newspaper that covered the local pop-music scene. That journal carried big stories on the Beatles, who were by this time arguably the top beat group in Liverpool.

Mersey Beat was published by Bill Harry, who had been at art college with John and Stu and had become good friends with them, especially Stu. He had been there when the Quarry Men had their lunchtime sessions at the college. It is not surprising then that from the first issue of the journal in July 1961 Harry incessantly plugged the already hugely popular Beatles. Brian, always trying to improve his business, got Harry to let him write a pop-record review column for the paper. He also placed ads in the paper. The column and ads appeared in the same issues of *Mersey Beat* that had the Beatles in banner headlines. He may not have been paying much attention, but Brian could hardly have not heard of the group.

It is true that as far as his business and column went, Brian was only interested in groups that made records, something most of the local beat groups had not done. So apparently not knowing that the Beatles were a local group—that he could have asked directly about the record—he went to Bill Harry for help. Harry informed him that not only were the Beatles not a German group, as Brian had thought, but that they in fact played regularly at the Cavern Club, which was only a few blocks from the NEMS department store where Brian worked.

It was no accident that Brian ran the record department at NEMS: his parents owned the store. But the success of the department was a result of Brian's bright mind and his will to succeed. At the time of his first contact with the Beatles he was a handsome, sensitive twenty-seven-year-old who had gone to good schools, but like the Beatles, did not take well to schooling. He also did not fit in well with other youngsters. He had always worked in the family business except for a brief stint in the army and a departure into theater. He was discharged from the army after only a few months because of his inability to adjust to army life.

Back in Liverpool, the theater soon beckoned. He had always loved the theater, and an acting career attracted him. Brian got involved with community theater in Liverpool and soon was hanging out with local actors. His theater friends thought he was talented and persuaded him to audition for the Royal Academy of Dramatic Art (RADA) in London. The academy accepted Brian, and for about a year he fared rather well in his training. This is not to be taken lightly, because his fellow acting students included such future stars as Susannah York, Albert Finney, and Peter O'Toole. But the reserved Brian grew tired of the actor's lifestyle. Hunter Davies quotes him as saying, "I just didn't like it, or any of the people. I began to think it was too late [for an acting career]. I was more a businessman after all." In 1957, he returned to the family business to follow a new calling in retail record sales.[1]

After he realized who the Beatles were, Epstein set out to find out more about the group's difficult-to-locate recording. Brian's interest was piqued when he asked some of the young shop girls if they had heard of the group, and he was astonished when he found that they not only had heard about them but were wild about them as well. He was further intrigued when he found out that the boys frequently visited the record department, and he had once thought of having them removed because of their scruffy, black-leather look. Brian's curiosity was now at a peak, and he really wanted to see the group in person. Of course, the Cavern Club was a teenage club, and he was nervous about going there and being out of place, so Harry arranged his visit with Bob Wooler, the club's DJ and compere.

On November 9, 1961, the well-dressed, dignified businessman, Brian Epstein, arrived at the Cavern Club. He walked down the steps into the steaming, dripping lunchtime chaos of the Cavern Club, packed to the rafters with screaming teenagers, mostly young girls. No matter that he was expected, he felt totally out of place. Jostled, bumped, and crushed, he felt immediately that it was a total mistake to have descended into this teenage hell. He was further embarrassed when Bob Wooler announced Mr. Epstein of NEMS records had arrived and asked the audience to give him a big hand. Feeling terribly conspicuous, the reserved Brian no doubt felt like crawling into one of the cracks in the Cavern Club's stony walls.

When the Beatles took the stage, he vaguely recalled their unkempt presence in his store. He was shocked not just by their disheveled appearance but by their stage presentation as well. He remembered that, "They smoked as they played and they ate and talked and pretended to hit each other. They turned their back on the audience and shouted at people and laughed at their private jokes." He could scarcely believe what he saw; he had never seen performers behave this way on stage. But he saw something else: "there was quite clearly an enormous excitement. They seemed to give off some sort of personal magnetism. I was fascinated by them."[2] He would later say in a radio interview, "I immediately liked what I heard. They were fresh and they were honest, and they had what I thought was a sort of presence and . . . star quality. Whatever that is . . . they had it."[3]

After their set, Brian made his way backstage. He wanted to find out more about their record, who produced it, and how he could get copies. Suddenly he found himself face to face with George, who reportedly said, "What brings Mr. Epstein here?"[4] It was a question that had a profound answer weeks later. But at that time Brian only wanted information. After he got what he wanted he left and immediately set about ordering two hundred copies of the record. Wooler had played the record for him, and he didn't think it was so great, but he could see the demand was there.

It could have just ended there; Brian thought that selling records was the only reason for his venture. He kept thinking about the group, however, and was truly fascinated. Now he found himself returning to the lunchtime sessions to catch their act again and again and became better acquainted with the group. They seemed to be so disorganized and directionless, but with so much raw talent. An idea began to germinate in his mind. He wasn't quite sure how or why, but somehow he believed that he could work with this group and help them progress. He had no experience with groups, but he felt a desire to guide them, and he was bored with the record business and ready for some new, challenging excitement in his life. And here were the Beatles. To mold, direct, and control their development became his passion.

It happened that the Beatles were also getting impatient with their status quo and were itching to move on. So when Brian proposed that they meet to discuss a business proposition they accepted. Neither party knew what to expect, really, but all were curious enough to find out. On December 3, 1961, this historic meeting took place in Brian's office. The boys brought Bob Wooler along to have an older, wiser voice with them, and John introduced him as his dad. Apparently, Brian did not realize they were not related until much later. They were all on time except Paul. After a bit, Brian, a stickler for punctuality, had George call Paul's home. It turned out Paul had taken a long bath and was on his way. Brian said angrily, "He's going to be very late." George responded wryly, "Yes, late, but very clean."

The meeting was just exploratory. Brian gave them an idea of what he might be able to do for them as manager of a major record store, who had some influence with record companies. They left that meeting agreeing that they would take three days to think on it and then meet again to see where they were. Brian sought some legal advice and even contacted Allan Williams for his opinion of managing the Beatles. The responses were all negative, of course, especially from Williams.

When they met again on December 6, Brian was a lot more specific about what he was proposing. He would take charge of everything—their bookings, fees (which would be increased), publicity, stage appearance, record deals—every aspect of their artistic lives. He would take 25 percent, a good fee, but necessary because of the risks he was taking, financial and otherwise. When he was done there was a brief awkward silence; then John, always the leader, leaned forward and said, "Right then Brian. Manage us. Now where's the contract, I'll sign it."[5]

From that time on, for all intents and purposes, Brian was the manager of the Beatles, and the actual signing of the contract later was a mere formality. In any case, that contract, the instrument that spurred the Beatles to fame, was never legal because Brian never signed it, a strange

Ships await unloading at the Liverpool docks. John, Paul, George, and Ringo grew up in Liverpool, a rough-and-tumble port city in northwestern England.

Three nattily attired teddy boys hang out on a street corner. The teds gained notoriety in England in the 1950s by inciting brawls in theaters, clubs, and other public meeting places.

Mimi Smith took this early photo of her nephew John Lennon. *Throughout his life, John maintained a sense of mischief and an attitude of rebellion.*

Paul McCartney performs as a Beatle. Paul and John combined creative forces to become the most successful songwriting team in the history of rock 'n' roll.

George Harrison pauses during a practice session in Hamburg, Germany. George was fifteen years old when he first played with John and Paul in a skiffle band called the Quarry Men.

In his pre-Beatles days, Ringo Starr mugs for the camera during a gig with Rory Storm and the Hurricanes.

Elvis Presley (above), Little Richard (at piano), Chuck Berry (right) set the house on fire in the late 1950s. These three American rockers were among the Beatles' main musical idols.

Johnny Gentle wows an audience in 1960. The Silver Beetles—John, Paul, George, bassist Stu Sutcliffe, and drummer Tommy Moore—were hired as the pop singer's band on a nine-day tour of Scotland that same year. It was their first taste of the big time.

Cliff Richard and the Shadows were immensely popular in England when the Beatles first burst on the nation's music scene. Looking and sounding nothing like Richard's band and its many imitators, the Beatles popularized a fresh style of music known as the Mersey beat.

George, Paul, and John twist and shout during a gig in Hamburg. The long, draining Hamburg performances polished their musical skills and taught them how to mach schau.

Stu Sutcliffe, the Beatles' original bass guitarist, died of a brain tumor in 1962. Paul took over at bass following Stu's death.

Astrid Kirchherr snapped this shot of the Beatles at the Hamburg Fun Fair in 1960. Pete Best (far left) was the band's drummer at the time.

Prior to a Beatles performance, Astrid Kirchherr (far right) joins young Liverpudlians queuing up outside the Cavern Club.

The Beatles rock the dank, dimly lit Cavern Club. From February 1962 to August 1963, the band played nearly 300 gigs at the subterranean club.

Brian Epstein became the Beatles' manager in 1961. He refined their image, got them a record deal, and helped turn the band into an international sensation.

*G*eorge Martin produced most of the Beatles' records. His talents helped the band create the perfect sound for the catchy pop songs of its early days and the complex, multilayered songs of its later period.

PLEASE PLEASE ME ★ THE BEATLES

PARLOPHONE

THE BEATLES

PLEASE
PLEASE ME

with Love Me Do
and 12 other songs

Parlophone released the Beatles' first album, Please Please Me, in March 1963. The album included their two hit singles, "Please Please Me" and "Love Me Do," and four other Lennon-McCartney originals. The album reached number one on the Melody Maker chart in six weeks.

omission for a person so detail fixated. Later Brian would say that if he weren't successful, he didn't want the boys bound to the contract. In his own mind he knew he would honor it to the letter. It was Paul who had a moment of doubt before signing. He asked if it would make any difference in the way they played, and Brian assured him that it would not.

In the larger sense, Brian never really interfered in what they wanted to do musically. But how it was presented, the image that they projected, concerned him very much. He did feel he should have some control over *what* they played. He encouraged them to stick to the best material in their repertoire and not just play anything on a whim. Furthermore, he wanted them to spruce up the act. No more smoking, swearing, and eating on stage.

Brian started booking them into larger and better clubs and halls, cutting down the length of performances and upping the price per performance. This was not a problem because the Beatles were in such high demand locally. He wanted them looking neat and tidy on stage; their rough, black-leather look was on the way out, and natty suits were on the way in. John later criticized Brian "for putting us in suits." While he preferred the leather look, which was a major part of the Beatles' early charm, Brian saw the big future picture, and as usual, he won out.

Although the Mersey beat sound was growing more popular all the time, surpassing all other musical styles in the area, there was still a dearth of publicity for local groups, which numbered in the hundreds. Even the top groups seldom got play in the Liverpool press, except for *Mersey Beat*, which concentrated largely on the local pop-music scene. Brian was doggedly determined to increase the Beatles' press coverage, but even he had difficulty cracking the seeming aloofness of local journals. Outside of Liverpool and Hamburg, the Beatles and other Merseyside groups were virtually unknown. It was going to take something more than an adoring fandom at the Cavern

Club to propel them to national fame, and Brian knew what it was: they needed a hit record.

Brian may have not had much clout with the press, but as one of the top record-sellers in Merseyside, he certainly rated some attention from the record companies. Decca was the first company to succumb to Brian's leverage. If nothing else they would at least listen to the group being touted by someone who moved a lot of their records. Decca dispatched an A and R (artists and repertoire) man to Liverpool to hear the Beatles perform at the Cavern Club. It was the first A and R man anyone could remember coming to the Cavern, and the atmosphere was electric. No question the Beatles had the home-field advantage, with their fans packed in and screaming for more. The Decca emissary had to be impressed. He arranged for the Beatles to come to London for an audition. It was December 1961, and they felt ready to soar.

Soar they did not, however; disappointment reigned instead. The audition came on New Year's Day 1962, and they all felt they had done well, and their hopes were high. They stuck mostly to standards on Brian's advice, abandoning for the most part their own material. Whether or not that was a mistake is something still not known, but it took two months for a Decca producer, after much prodding by Brian, to finally say no, Mr. Epstein, they did not like the group's sound. He added, "Groups of guitarists are on the way out." Despite Brian's insistence that the boys were about to explode and that "one day they will be bigger than Elvis Presley," Decca remained firm.[6] It was the largest single mistake ever made in that company's history and probably the largest in the recording industry's history. In the 1990s, Beatles record receipts are heading toward the billion-dollar mark.

The news that Decca had turned them down hit the boys especially hard because everything else was going so well. Not only were they playing better venues for more money, but they also signed a new and more rewarding contract to go back to Hamburg, and they had recorded their first BBC radio broadcast on March 7. Furthermore, they had won the *Mersey Beat* popularity poll in January, naming them the top beat group in Merseyside. Still, they needed a record to go to the next level.

Brian, despite the Decca setback, continued his quest for a recording contract. All the record companies he approached made the same mistake that Decca had, turning him down. He became quite discouraged but decided to make one last all-out assault on the London recording firms. His father, who was his boss after all, wanted him back in the store attending to business, and Brian felt his time to find a record contract was just about up.

In London, Brian made a fateful decision that changed the direction of his and the Beatles' lives. He decided in London to make a vinyl record of the tapes he had been carrying around to record companies. A record, he thought, might somehow be more appealing to record-company executives. He used the facilities at a record outlet owned by EMI, the giant recording conglomerate, to make the record. There, a recording technician liked the music so much that he contacted an executive of the EMI record outlet, who in turn recommended it to a music publisher. The publisher, indeed, liked the music, said he would like to publish some of it and would recommend Brian to a contact at Parlophone, a minor recording subsidiary of EMI. The man at Parlophone was a moderately successful A and R man who was classically trained and knew little, if anything, about rock 'n' roll. His name was George Martin, and he turned out to be the golden link.

The Beatles in the meantime were off to Hamburg. Before they left there had been disquieting news: Stu, who was in residence there with Astrid, was not well. He had been having severe headaches, and no one could determine the cause. When they got off the plane (Brian insisted they travel in style), Astrid was there to greet them. The distraught look on her face that April morning in 1962 immediately told them the bad news: Stu, twenty-one years old, was dead of a brain hemorrhage. He had died in her arms while heading for the hospital in an ambulance. The boys were devastated. Despite the record company disappointments, they had been generally upbeat about the way things were going. There were some minor disputes with Brian, but the boys realized that his management had definitely taken them to another level. Now, for the moment, it seemed like their world was torn apart. Pete Best said in his autobiography, "We . . . didn't try to hide the tears welling into our eyes. John, who had been closer to Stu than Paul or me, wept like a child. I had never seen him break down in public like this before."[7]

On this trip, the Beatles were engaged to open the Star Club, a large, completely modern venue that eclipsed their previous playing sites. It was clearly the class of the Reeperbahn, and the boys felt privileged to have been chosen as the inaugural group. Their popularity in Hamburg, if anything, was even greater than in Liverpool. Recovering from the grief of Stu's death, they soon returned to the raucous lifestyle of their previous visits to Hamburg. Because their popularity was greater than ever, they had a better cash flow and could enjoy the nightlife of Hamburg more than ever, as well as the company of Astrid and her "exis" crowd. Playing until 4:00 A.M. and then having dates after that, they generally fell into an exhausted sleep until midday.

It was on a morning early in May that they were awoken from their deep slumber by a knock at the door. George answered. It was a telegram from Brian, which he tore open and read to the group: "Congratulations, boys, EMI request recording session. Please rehearse new material."[8]

The world of pop music was about to explode.

THE CONQUEST BEGINS

The obvious was the last thing they wanted. Ever.
—George Martin, quoted in the *New Yorker*, November 20, 1995

Brian and George Martin of Parlophone hit it off right from the start. Both were refined and well educated, and Brian was certainly not like the other huckstering managers that came pounding at Martin's door. More than likely Martin found it refreshing to deal with someone of Brian's quiet intelligence. None of that would have mattered, however, if he had not heard something in the Beatles' recordings that struck him. Martin had produced mostly comedy records and some refined pop music, but no rock. Nevertheless, Martin's ear for music was highly regarded. He was a trained classical musician and an established arranger and composer as well. He said to Brian, "I know very little about groups, Brian, but I believe you have something very good here."[1]

Martin may not have totally understood what he heard, but he felt it was worth a crack and agreed with Brian to set up a recording test. Here, at least, was a sound that he thought was fresh and original. The test was set for June 6, 1962. The Beatles were ecstatic to get the news, never having hoped that a prestigious company such as EMI would make them an offer, even if it was the

Parlophone label. They were anxious to get back, but first they had to wind up their engagement at the Star Club, which they did on May 31. Now traveling in style, they flew back to England and managed a couple days off and a rehearsal before embarking to London on June 4.

The first recording session, more of an audition really, took place a couple of days later at EMI's Abbey Studios, which would become famous as the site of the Beatles' blockbuster recordings. Now the Beatles and George Martin met face to face, and he was immediately charmed by their wit and felt their energy and chemistry, as Brian had. The Beatles were equally impressed by George Martin—suave, sophisticated, and knowledgeable. Also they were terribly impressed that he had worked with some of their favorite comedy stars, such as Peter Sellers.

It may have been Martin's ear for comedy that also enforced his attraction to the group. Their dry, off-the-wall Liverpudlian humor was always breaking out. At this first meeting he oriented the Beatles to the intricacies of recording and gave them numerous instructions. Afterward, as they sat silentl and unreactive, Martin said, "Let me know if there is anything you don't like." The Beatles sat expressionless for a moment, and then George piped up, "Well for a start, I don't like your tie." That cracked everyone up; they all relaxed, and the session began.[2]

The Beatles on that day recorded at least four songs for Martin's test. These included "Besame Mucho" and three Lennon-McCartney originals: "Love Me Do," "P.S. I Love You," and "Ask Me Why." Martin was noncommittal after the session, but Brian and the Beatles felt good about what they had done and were optimistic. This time they were not disappointed. In late July, Brian signed a contract with Parlophone and Martin, who knew he wanted them but wasn't quite sure why. They were to return in early September to make final recordings, two of which would be chosen for their first single. The boys, who had been playing almost nonstop gigs since their first session with Martin, were in a state of euphoria.

While they were in Hamburg, Brian had booked them solidly into September, still mostly in Merseyside. Their first stop was, as might be expected, the Cavern Club, where they had a welcome-home night and smashed the club attendance record. Lines stretched down the street for both the early and late shows. A couple of days later they were off to Manchester to record their second BBC radio broadcast. After the show they were nearly mobbed in the streets as they made their way back to their bus. Pete Best, at that time, seemed to get the most attention. Now their popularity had spread beyond Liverpool, and fans were sprouting up in other northern cities.

Through June, July, and August they continued to play the Cavern at least several times a week while mixing in dates at nearby prestigious ballrooms and clubs. Venues included the Tower Ballroom in New Brighton, the Plaza Ballroom in St. Helens, the Majestic Ballroom in Birkenhead, and Cambridge Hall in Southport. On several programs they got second billing to such nationally known headliners as Bruce Channel, who had a top-ten hit; Gene Vincent, who had had several hits; and Joe Brown, who had a number-three hit. It was Brian's idea to have the Beatles appear with these giants to get the added exposure and press coverage and hopefully even outshine them and draw more attention to themselves.[3]

August was a particularly momentous month for the Beatles because of two highly significant events. For one, during this month Cyn told John she was pregnant. At the time, neither birth control nor abortion were readily available. In any case, John, with his background of parental abandonment, was not about to forsake his own child. The usually unflappable John was shaken at first by the news, but he recovered quickly, looked his high-school sweetheart in the eye, and said, "Don't worry Cyn, we'll get married." And so they did, on August 23, 1962. John had been with Cyn since high school, but with his career going bang on, marriage was not really in his plans. Nevertheless, John was determined to be a good father. The child, Julian Lennon, was born April 8, 1963.

There was some fear that the news of John's marriage would affect the group's popularity because their fan following was mostly young teenage girls who had crushes on them. Already each had his own cultlike following. There was some speculation that they might even break up, but no such thing happened. They were building momentum, and it seemed like nothing could slow them down at this point.

The other momentous event of August 1962 probably had an even more telling effect on their careers. It happened on August 16, 1962. The night before, Brian had given a message to Pete Best that he wanted a meeting with him the next morning. When Pete showed up in Brian's office, the Beatles' manager passed a few pleasantries then dropped the bombshell: "The boys want you out and Ringo in." Pete was so stunned he could barely speak. When he was told that Ringo had already accepted their offer to become a Beatle, he surmised that a conspiracy had taken place. And it had.[4]

Many versions of Pete's sacking arose after it happened, and speculation goes on to this day. After he gave Pete the news, Brian, also emotionally wrought, added a brief explanation: "They don't think you're a good enough drummer, Pete. And George Martin doesn't think you're a good enough drummer." Probably that was the heart of the matter; most authorities would likely agree that Pete was not the greatest drummer, although there was a faction that thought Pete was the best drummer in Merseyside—better than Ringo. Pete certainly felt he was the better drummer and even claimed that Ringo copied his big-beat style. But it was Ringo who had been chosen to record with the Beatles in Hamburg, and it was Ringo who had been lured away from Rory Storm to back Tony Sheridan in Hamburg. Some rock scholars even regard Ringo as the drummer who set the style for rock drummers in the decades to come.

Brian, in his autobiography, says that he was against dismissing Pete. He was nervous about changing the chemistry of the group when it all seemed to be going so well. "I asked the Beatles to leave the group as it was," he wrote. They were adamant, however, and wanted his departure "sooner or later" for reasons besides his drumming. Brian explained, "They thought him too conventional to be a Beatle and though he was friendly with John, he was not liked by George and Paul. And one night . . . the three of them . . . demanded, 'We want Pete out and Ringo in.' "[5]

Jealousy was another possibility, although the Beatles discounted this and Pete himself seemed unable to accept this in his autobiography. It is true though that Pete was sometimes depicted as the group leader and as the most popular Beatle. Indeed, he did have something of a mystique with his sullen good looks. As such, the girls went for Pete, and he was sometimes mobbed by them more than the others. Regarding the jealousy theory, Paul told Hunter Davies, "I wasn't jealous of [Best] because he was handsome. That's all junk. He just couldn't play. Ringo was so much better."[6]

Pete's popularity was borne out by the fierce reaction to the firing once the news got out. BEATLES CHANGE DRUMMER! screamed a headline in *Mersey Beat*. The article quoted the Beatles as saying that the separation was "entirely amicable," although it was anything but. Near riots, protests, petitions, and denunciations ensued, with Brian as the main villain, but the other four (including Ringo) all taking some of the flak. At the Cavern, the crowds shouted, "We want Pete," or "Pete forever, Ringo never." At one point the boys were mobbed, and George suffered a black eye, which was still evident at the recording session in September. All fan protestation was for naught; Ringo took over the drums on August 19 at the Cavern Club.[7]

It is generally agreed that Pete's sacking was handled rather shoddily, and even Brian and the Beatles later admitted as much. The events were all the more surprising since Brian was usually noted for his tact. He did offer Pete some other opportunities (Brian by this time was also representing other groups), but Pete refused, hooking up instead with Lee Curtis and the All-Stars, who became, for a time, the number-two Liverpool group behind the Beatles.

After the furor died down Ringo Starr slipped right into place as the Beatles' drummer as though nature had dictated it. He shaved his beard and cut his hair in Beatle style (which Pete had refused to do), blending his physical appearance with that of the rest of the group. He immediately offered a more lively presence at the drum station. The Beatles now felt that they had a drummer who could record with them. Not quite! When they showed up in London on September 4, George Martin had barely heard of the drummer switch. He hadn't cared that much for Pete Best, but who was Ringo?

After the first set of recordings, which included "Love Me Do" and a Mitch Murray composition, "How Do You Do It," Martin decided he had better hire a regular studio, or session, drummer to sit in with the boys. At another session on September 11, the boys recorded the same numbers and others, including "P.S. I Love You," with Ringo sometimes relegated to the maracas and tambourine. Ringo was crushed by this treatment, but it would not happen again.

Martin at first decided he wanted "How Do You Do It," which he thought would be a sure hit, to be on their first single, but the boys objected furiously. They wanted instead to do their own material. In the end Martin gave in, selecting "Love Me Do" for the A side and "P.S. I Love You" for the B side. Surprisingly, the "Love Me Do" version he picked was from the earlier session with Ringo on drums. That made Ringo exceedingly happy, and, perhaps, it said something about Martin's musical flexibility. The B side had Ringo on the maracas. On October 5, 1963, the Beatles' first record was released, and from that day their mercurial rise to fame and fortune was begun.

By late December, the record had reached number seventeen on one of the British charts. It was the first time a Liverpool beat group had made a record that climbed into the charts. Indeed, the Liverpool beat groups were hardly known outside of Merseyside, except for the Beatles, who now had a glimmer of a national reputation. Martin, incidentally, was vindicated in his preference for "How Do You Do It" when that song, performed by Gerry and the Pacemakers (also managed by Brian), reached number one the next year. Martin was the producer.

Brian continued to upgrade the Beatles' live-performance venues, while they also continued to draw overflow crowds at the Cavern. October 12 was a particularly satisfying date for the group. On that date Brian promoted an all-star rock spectacular at the New Brighton Tower Ballroom that included one of the great booking coups in the city's history. The Beatles' own idol, Little Richard, headlined the bill with the Beatles, now EMI recording stars, in the number-two spot. October 28 was another red-letter day because they played the prestigious Liverpool Empire Theatre, again on a bill starring Little Richard.

The pace was now quickening for the Beatles, who were playing almost every day, but it was child's play compared to what was to come. They continued to make recordings for radio broadcasts, including the BBC's *Here We Go* and Radio Luxembourg's *The Friday Spectacular*, and made some television inroads, appearing several times on the variety show *People and Places* before the end of the year. A film crew even tried to shoot a show in the Cavern Club, but the light was so bad that the footage was not used until the Beatles were much more famous and any vintage Beatles clip was in great demand.

On November 1, it was back to Hamburg for another two-week stint at the Star Club. They returned to Liverpool for a continuous string of engagements at the Cavern Club and other local sites. George Martin, quite satisfied with the progress of "Love Me Do," beckoned them again to the recording studio on November 26. Their next single was "Please Please Me" and "Ask Me Why," both Lennon-McCartney compositions. George Martin had asked them to rearrange "Please Please Me," and after the session he said, "Gentlemen, you've made your first number one record." The accuracy of that prophesy would soon vindicate Martin's faith in the Beatles, who themselves were pleased that Martin had bowed to their insistence on recording their own material.[8]

Things were now really rolling for Brian Epstein. By December, the Beatles had been heard nationally on radio and television, usually plugging "Love Me Do" and "P.S. I Love You," and on October 27 their first single had hit the *Melody Maker* singles chart in the forty-eighth position. There were rumors that Brian had bought up huge quantities of the record to lift its chart position, but he denied buying any more than what he needed to sell in his own record stores. The London press took small note of them but at this point was not too impressed. Taking advantage of their improving national position, Brian managed to book them on a prominent national tour with one of Britain's top stars, Helen Shapiro. The tour started in February 1963 and played almost every major venue in the country.

Just for a warm-up, the tour promoter asked if the Beatles would be available in early December for a one-night appearance at another major show featuring an Australian pop star named Frank Ifield. Brian gratefully agreed; even though the boys would make only expense money, they would still be performing with a national star on a major stage, the Empire Cinema in Peterborough.

What nobody had realized at the time was that the Beatles and Frank Ifield were apples and oranges: Ifield was a schmaltzy, yodeling ballad singer, and the Beatles were rock 'n' roll. The date was one of the few in which the Beatles bombed. The audience hadn't the foggiest grasp of what the Beatles were doing, and a local reviewer, while praising Ifield, said the "exciting Beatles' rock group quite frankly failed to excite me. The drummer apparently thought his job was to lead. . . . He made far to much noise . . . and in their final number 'Twist and Shout' it sounded as though everyone was trying to make more noise than the others." The Beatles found out that you can't please everybody.[9]

In mid-December, the Beatles returned to Hamburg for a fifth and final romp. They were reluctant to go, and they could hardly be blamed. Hamburg and the Star Club were old stuff for them, and in Britain things were just starting to heat up on a national scale. They were on television and radio, and they had a record out that hit pretty high in the charts and another one about to burst onto the scene. It was no time to be in Hamburg, even though their fee had been considerably improved. A contract was a contract, however, and Brian saw to it that it was honored. It was during this last frolic at the Star Club that John came on for one performance wearing a toilet seat around his neck. The Beatles had not forgotten how to *mach schau*.

TO THE TOP OF THE CHARTS

Yeah, Yeah, Yeah.

—from "She Loves You" by Lennon-McCartney

The Beatles finally exploded fully onto the national scene in 1963. They had achieved some notoriety from their first record and a few radio and television broadcasts, but London had still hardly taken notice of them. The question now was whether their first release, which had reached number seventeen, was a flash in the pan or whether it would be followed with similar success by their next record. After a quick tour of Scotland to start the year, they released "Please Please Me" / "Ask Me Why" on January 11. On that date the Beatles were booked on the television show *Thank Your Lucky Stars*, a perfectly timed appearance for plugging their new single.

"Please Please Me" blew the lid off. Unlike "Love Me Do," which had erratic success, this single rose steadily to the top of the charts, hitting number one on the *New Musical Express* charts on February 22 and on the *Melody Maker* charts on March 2. The news hit the Beatles while they were on tour with the remarkable Helen Shapiro, a sixteen-year-old who had been acclaimed as the top female British singer for the previous two years. Brian and the Beatles went bonkers, and George Martin was beginning to believe he had found Parlophone's answer to Cliff Richards and the Shadows, whose hit records had been the envy of the record industry.

The Beatles were now able to do something about their own success, playing top venues throughout Britain and plugging their singles at every stop. Aside from the tour with Helen Shapiro, which ended March 3, they played other gigs, including the Cavern (their appearances there now becoming somewhat rare), and were being heard on radio and television. Even before the boys' new single hit number one, Brian and George saw the Beatles' popularity growing by leaps and bounds on a national basis, and they wanted to feed the flames. George Martin called for another studio session on February 11, this time to record the Beatles' first album. Two singles and an album all in a space of a few months; on tour with a national celebrity; radio and television demanding appearances regularly; where was this headed?

Neither the Beatles, Brian, nor George could have possibly guessed what lay ahead. But perhaps the fans could, those who were starting to cause disturbances wherever the Beatles showed up, especially if they couldn't get tickets. It was becoming common for hundreds to be turned away at their shows.

The album was entitled *Please Please Me*, and it included both their singles and four other Lennon-McCartney compositions in addition to six nonoriginal songs. All the recorded material was part of their regular repertoire, so little rehearsal was needed. Nevertheless, that they were able to record the album in one studio session was nothing short of astonishing. But with their pressing concert schedule, they had little choice. They had been playing and singing for more than twelve hours when they got to the last cut, the demanding "Twist and Shout," in which John sings the lead and must let loose several primal screams. "John and his voice were pretty shot," said George Martin. "As 'Twist and Shout' is a hell of a singing thing John had to really get it in one take."[1] And he did. Although not a Beatles original, "Twist and Shout" had become closely associated with the group and was often used to end concerts sensationally.

Two other blockbuster hits came out of the album: "I Saw Her Standing There" and "Do You Want to Know a Secret," both Lennon-McCartney originals. The album was released March 22 and was an almost immediate smash. It started at number ten on the *Melody Maker* album charts; by May 4 it was number one, and it remained on the charts for an amazing thirty-week run. Brian was right: a hit record was what they needed to break out. But this was just the beginning.

Riding the crest of their first two major hit records, in April the Beatles cut yet a third single, "From Me to You" / "Thank You Girl." Again they were Lennon-McCartney songs, and it was becoming apparent that George Martin was now offering little resistance to the boys doing their own material. The latest single was released on April 20, and it took only two weeks for it to hit number one, holding that spot for six weeks. It looked as though they might be as hot as Cliff Richards—maybe hotter. They might have been the hottest recording artists in Britain. But Brian and George did not want the well to go dry and did not release an EP (extended play) "Twist and Shout" until July and their fourth single, "She Loves You"/ "I'll Get You" until late August.

Even when the Beatles were not recording, Lennon-McCartney songs were being recorded by other artists, particularly those also being managed by Brian, who was building a stable of top-flight talent. One of these was Billy J. Kramer, who recorded several Lennon-McCartney numbers and had a hit with "Do You Want to Know a Secret." Another Brian talent, and an old friend of the Beatles from the early Cavern Club days, was Cilla Black, who recorded John and Paul's "Love of the Loved."

Through spring and early summer of 1963, the Beatles

were in constant motion. When not in the studio, they were on tour, playing almost daily and appearing on radio and television. The schedule was incredibly grueling, with Brian driving the boys at breakneck speed. John barely had time to take off April 8 for the birth of his son Julian, who was named for John's mother, Julia. He and the boys played a Cavern Club gig the following night.

Before Julian's birth, the group had just finished their second tour with American artists Chris Montez and Tommy Roe, taking third billing. A helper on the tour told stories of "smashed up hotel rooms and fights on the coach." In his opinion, "They probably got fed up getting 100 pounds a week when they were drawing the crowd."[2] It was the first time in memory that British pop stars outshined Americans on the same bill, and it was the last tour on which the Beatles would not take top billing.

The Beatles occasionally played dates in London but were still not getting much attention from the London press despite their recent hit records and growing national notoriety. The fact that people were flocking to see them just wasn't registering in the mainstream print media and, thus, on much of British society. After a brief break in Spain and the Canary Islands, without which they may have collapsed, the Beatles went on another tour, their third in less than half a year.

This time they were on a bill that was supposed to be headed by an American singer, Roy Orbison, who had been hot for several years in Britain. Between the time of the booking and the actual tour, however, the Beatles had grown even hotter, and they felt they should be the show closer. Orbison disapproved, but by this time the Beatles were clearly the more popular act and they prevailed. Bewildered, the innocent American asked, "What is a Beatle, anyway?" John Lennon tapped him on the shoulder and said, "I'm one."[3]

While on tour with Orbison, George made a revelation that gave rise to a Beatle tradition—one that they wished had never begun. George told an interviewer that he loved jelly babies (jelly beans), and from that time forward Beatle fans showered their idols with the candy wherever they appeared.

On this tour they also came to understand the phrase "a tough act to follow." Orbison's fans turned out in large numbers, and maybe trying to prove something, he really put on a show. His fans applauded wildly and screamed for more. The Beatles, the next act on, fretted. Ringo later said, "It was terrible following him, he'd slay them . . . just doing it by his voice. Just standing there singing, not moving or anything. He was knocking them out. . . . We would hide behind the curtain, whispering . . . guess who's next folks, it's your favorite rave."[4] In the end, of course, they would go out and wow the audience.

The whirlwind pace continued through July and August. Everywhere the Beatles went they drew huge, rambunctious, jelly-belly–throwing crowds. Although the London press was not giving them much shrift, local papers were taking note of their incredible popularity, and their faces were plastered across the covers of all the pop-music magazines. Security and safety was getting to be a problem, and extra hands had to be hired to keep them from being trounced. An official fan club had been established in Liverpool, and branches were being set up in other cities throughout Britain. A magazine devoted entirely to the Beatles, the *Beatles Book* published its first issue in August.

That month was marked by two other landmark events, one happy, one sad. The happy event was the release of their fourth single, "She Loves You" / "I'll Get You." The A side, "She Loves You," was the first song in which the Beatles chanted their now-famous chorus of "Yeah, Yeah, Yeah." It caught on like wildfire, and soon other groups were echoing the same phrase, and all Britain echoed with "Yeah, Yeah, Yeah." The record shot right up the charts.

The sad event of August 1963 was the Beatles' final gig

at the Cavern Club. No one was surprised that they never returned after August 3. Their fees were too high, and it was getting more and more difficult to get back to Liverpool. They just had grown too big for small clubs, especially the Cavern where the audience was jammed right up to the stage. Often half-crazed fans reached out, grasping for a touch, a piece of their clothes, their hair, a kiss, any possible contact. Protecting them was becoming a logistical nightmare.

The Cavern, along with Hamburg, had been the crucible of the Beatles' musical style, the place where they had honed their skills and where they had drawn their first devoted fans. They had played almost three hundred performances there, but now it was time to move on, and the fans understood and so did the whole city. For now Liverpool was on the map, not only as the home of the Beatles, but as the place where the Mersey sound was born. The Beatles, with Brian Epstein, had broken down the door for the Liverpool beat groups, and by the fall of 1963 their music was the rage of Britain.

Merseyside was supporting literally hundreds of rock 'n' roll groups by the time the Beatles had achieved national recognition. The area's teeming music culture was also enriched by dozens of groups and individual performers in the country-and-western, blues, and folk genres. They played in clubs, in coffee houses, in cellars, in theaters, and in halls of every kind. Several of the Liverpool groups broke out of the pack to achieve varying degrees of national and even international success, although none rivaled the Beatles. But then neither could any other group in Britain or in the world, for that matter.

Gerry and the Pacemakers were acknowledged as the number-two beat group in Liverpool, and they almost matched the Beatles' success for awhile. Recognizing their potential, Brian Epstein had contracted to manage the Pacemakers, and by the end of 1963 they were riding a wave of popularity driven by such hits as "How Do You Do

It," "I Like It," and "You'll Never Walk Alone." The group in fact had their first number-one hit, "How Do You Do It," before the Beatles had theirs.

Brian also signed up Billy J. Kramer after he reached number three in the *Mersey Beat* poll. Merging Kramer with a group called the Dakotas, Brian had them record several Lennon-McCartney songs, including "Do You Want to Know a Secret" and "Bad to Me," which hit number one on the British charts. Two other Brian Epstein properties also became successful: The Fourmost ("A Little Loving") and the solo singer, Cilla Black ("Anyone Who Had a Heart"). The Searchers were another leading Liverpool proponent of the Mersey beat, hitting high on the charts with such hits as "Sweets For My Sweet" and "Sugar and Spice." Other Liverpool groups that gained prominence included The Swinging Bluejeans ("The Hippy Hippy Shake") and The Merseybeats ("Its Love That Really Counts").

But the rampaging Beatles were in the lead and would never be caught. They continued their musical onslaught into the fall. In September, George Martin once again called them into the studio, this time to record their second album. For this cutting, seven of the numbers were Lennon-McCartney originals and one was a George Harrison original, "Don't Bother Me." The Lennon-McCartney contributions included such hits as "All My Loving" and "I Wanna Be Your Man." Among the other songs on the album were their highly popular rendition of "Roll Over Beethoven," written by a Beatles' idol, the American rock 'n' roller Chuck Berry, and Paul's tender rendering of "'Til There Was You," by Meredith Willson. The second album was called *With the Beatles*.

The Beatles' popularity climbed to even greater heights in September. *Melody Maker* magazine put out a special issue, *Big Beat Boys*, which honored Merseyside music and had the Beatles gracing the cover. At their performances throughout Britain the crowds continued to grow, and the first signs of related side-industries appeared; items such as collarless Beatles jackets hit the marketplace in English cities, and Beatles haircuts were beginning to pop up. The group found their way into increasingly prestigious venues, including London's Royal Albert Hall, where they headed a twelve-act show. On the same bill was another group that was starting to gain prominence and with whom the Beatles were to become quite friendly. They called themselves the Rolling Stones.[5]

This hyperactivity was being fueled by their latest single release, "She Loves You," which hit the top of the *Melody Maker* singles chart on September 7. It went on to become the Beatles' first million-selling gold record and the largest selling single in British history.[6] "Yeah, Yeah, Yeah" appeared to be a good idea.

Strangely enough, some of the hidebound London press still would not fully acknowledge the Beatles phenomenon, despite all that was crashing down about them. The fact that the Beatles had the top-selling single, EP, and album in the country still did not seem to make much difference. A rather long interview with the Beatles appeared in the *Daily Mirror*, but it treated them as a moneymaking curiosity. A later retrospective in the *Sunday Express* reported that "the tradition-bound Press still couldn't see the story. The papers remained blind to the social upheaval which the foursome were proliferating."[7]

It was the booking Brian obtained for October 13, 1963, that finally served as the wake-up call to the press. This would be their most prestigious gig yet. They were to head the bill on Britain's top-rated variety show at the London Palladium, which would be televised live nationwide. An estimated fifteen million viewers would watch the show. But the real story was outside the auditorium. There the crowds gathered, numbering into thousands, most of whom were teen-age girls screaming, "we want the Beatles." The police were taken by surprise and had to bring in reserves to control the hysteria. The media could not ignore this spectacle, and reporters and news cameramen from rival stations rushed to cover the story. The noise of screaming fans outside was so loud that it could be heard through the Palladium walls. And of course the noise inside was equally intense.

The next day the press did indeed take note. All of the major papers ran front-page stories, not so much about the music, but about the phenomena of the event.[8] SIEGE OF THE BEATLES screamed a headline in the *Daily Herald*. According to the story, "Screaming girls launched themselves against the police sending helmets flying and constables reeling." When the Beatles left, they were smuggled into their car by the police, but the crowd could not be held back. "The teenagers charged forward and the Beatles' car went off into Oxford street chased by the crowd."

One reporter coined a term to describe the event. He called it "Beatlemania." Yes, indeed it was—loosed full-blown upon the British public.

BEATLEMANIA ASCENDING

Beatlemania descended on the British Isles in October 1963. . . . It didn't lift for three years, by which time it had spread and had covered the whole world. There was a perpetual screaming and yeh-yehing for three years, one long continuous succession of hysterical teenagers of every class and color, shouting uncontrollably, not one of whom could hear what was going on for the noise of each other. Each of them emotionally, mentally, or sexually excited, foaming at the mouth, bursting into tears, hurling themselves like lemmings in the direction of the Beatles or just simply fainting.

It is impossible to exaggerate Beatlemania because Beatlemania was in itself an exaggeration.

—Hunter Davies, *The Beatles:*
The Authorized Biography

Some authorities contend that Beatlemania in Britain was an event waiting to happen. For months, the country had been reeling from a major sex and security scandal, the so-called Profumo Affair, which involved a high-ranking government official, John Profumo, and his affair with model Christine Keeler. The Beatles came along at the right time and seemed to clear the air of the murky, depressing hangover left from the day-to-day newspaper reports of the seamy affair. So it is probably no surprise that the distraction of four happy-go-lucky, charming minstrels setting the country on its ear was just the tonic the British needed.

Hardly had the hullabaloo from the Palladium gig died down when a new excitement was created: the announcement of a booking that even topped the Palladium. The Beatles were invited to play at the Royal Variety Performance, a charity show which would be attended by the queen and other members of the royal family. Playing before the queen! For a Briton it was the highest conceivable honor. But the four tough lads from Liverpool were not particularly impressed. What did give them a bit of a kick was seeing their name on the bill with such a lustrous personality as the glamorous movie star Marlene Dietrich, even though they topped her on the bill.[1] Ringo did tell one reporter that he would like to play for the Queen Mother. Interestingly, the Beatles, perhaps because of their humble backgrounds, never again accepted an invitation to play at the annual royal affair.

Before the Beatles were to fill their date with the queen, they had another quite enthralling tour to make. This one would take them overseas again on their first visit to Sweden. They had become quite popular in that country, their fame now spreading beyond the British Isles, and Swedish teenagers were buying up every ticket in sight. Their records had captivated the young people of that country, even though many could not understand what the Beatles were singing.

The Swedish tour, during the last week of October 1963, was just as demanding as their British tours. The boys did nine shows and made recordings for Swedish television and radio. The security logistics had to be just as tight as in Britain because Beatlemania was intense there, too. Police had to guard the Beatles wherever they went, but they could not always control the seething, delirious crowds. Stockholm may have been the worst. There the crazed, teenage audience broke through the police cordon and stormed the stage; George was trounced and almost carried off before police could clear the stage and restore order. Outside the theater, police had to use dogs to hold the crowd back.

Their return to the United Kingdom was a defining moment for the Beatles. Somehow in all the whirlwind of activity they had not themselves fully taken stock of who and what they had become. That revelation finally hit home when their plane from Sweden landed at the London airport. Thousands of screaming fans were there waiting to greet them in a drenching rain. The entire airport was tied up. Police, reporters, and cameramen were everywhere. Even the prime minister's car could not get through the chaos. From that point on, the airport scene was repeated again and again in London and wherever else the Beatles landed.[2]

After their arrival, only a few days remained before their royal performance on November 4. Not that they had a break at all, pushing off on a nationwide tour on November 1. They would break off from the tour to do the Royal Variety Performance, which was to be held at the Prince of Wales Theatre in London. That night, the scene at the theater was the same as it was at every other venue. The presence of the royal family had no restraining effect whatsoever on the Beatles fans who gathered outside the theater screaming for their idols. Constables had to form a solid line to withstand the force of the crowd hoping for any glimpse of a Beatle. Inside it was somewhat more subdued, the extremely high ticket price and the royal presence determining the character of the audience.

The Beatles were not intimidated, but they were respectful. In any case, Brian's tutelage had made them a far more refined and civil group than the foursome of the Hamburg *mach schau* days. They had cleaned up their act. Still, Brian had trepidations knowing that John, especially, could lose control at any time. There was at least one tense moment. Before playing "Twist and Shout," John made an announcement: "For this number we would like your help. Will the people in the cheaper seats clap your hands. All the rest of you [glancing at the royal box] just rattle your jewelry."[3] It was a jibe at the bejeweled royalty, but it was taken in the proper spirit. The straitlaced Brian was relieved because John had earlier threatened to insert some obscenities into the statement.

If the Beatles weren't already over the edge of mass appeal, the royal performance gave them the final push. In Britain, when you hobnob with the queen, you have achieved utter respectability. Now the press would not leave them alone and reported their every move. If a Beatle sneezed, it made the news. Back on tour, every stampede for tickets, the screaming and fainting at concerts, and the extreme strategies required to get the band in and out of theaters safely became the daily, usually front-page, fare of the media. The boys took more and more to disguises to get about safely. After one show they had to disguise themselves as constables with helmets and nightsticks in order to elude the crowd. Some members of Parliament objected to the cost to the public of the police protection required to insure the Beatles' safety.

In late November, the Beatles' second album, *With the Beatles*, and their fifth single, "I Want to Hold Your Hand" / "This Boy," were released. The album was an almost instant number one, with a British record-breaking advance order and sales of more than 500,000 copies in its first week. The single's popularity was equally astonishing. With an advanced order of close to a million (also a record), it entered the *Melody Maker* singles chart at number one. By the first week of December the Beatles held five positions in Britain's top twenty, including one and two. They were now the most popular recording artists in British history, and they were the most popular live entertainers as well. However, despite the thousands of pounds each was making every week, some of the fun was being drained out of the life they had been so eager to embrace.

To begin with, their lives had become a nonstop merry-go-round. They were doing two shows every day when they weren't recording or appearing on radio and television and were being interviewed when they weren't doing anything else. The intense pressure was beginning to take its toll. Getting in and out of theaters safely was a logistical nightmare, and they were growing tired of being in constant danger of bodily harm. Wearing disguises was also beginning to lose its novelty, and there was concern for the music itself. For all their fame, money, and prestige, they felt their music was being lost in the shuffle, at least in concerts.

The Beatles had always taken pride in their work, and playing was really important to them. But now at concerts they were no longer being heard. The crowd noise, the incessant screaming, was drowning them out. It was bad enough that no one could hear their music, but even worse, that they themselves could not hear what they were playing. Often they could not hear the count so they could not even start playing at the same time. They couldn't tell how well they were playing, and they feared their music would suffer.

Perhaps the worst of it, though, was being unable to go anywhere or do anything. It was impossible to ever leave their dressing rooms or their hotel rooms because of the impassioned mobs outside. They were virtually imprisoned by their own fame.[4]

Britain itself had become tiresome, and the boys were starting to itch to move out of the routine tours of Britain. Ever the planner and strategist, Brian was already setting his sights on great new adventures. One of these would be the cinema: it was announced in December that a film starring the Beatles would be made in 1964. John and Paul were also commissioned to write the music for a ballet called *Mods and Rockers*. But the really big news was that the boys would be setting out to conquer new worlds in 1964. The first of these would be France, where they would be touring during January. Then, in the following month, they would reach their highest pinnacle yet: their first United States visit.

It was really exciting news, but the Beatles and Brian were more than a little of fearful of how they would be received in America. History gave them reason to be fearful. British rock groups, despite their degree of success in their homeland, had generally fallen on their faces in the United States. Even with the Beatles setting British records in disc sales, Capitol Records, an American company, had steadfastly refused to issue a Beatles record. And Capitol was even owned by EMI, the British company that produced the Beatles recordings at Parlophone. Capitol would not budge even as the enormity of the Beatles' success hit them in the face.

Already there had been some minor skirmishes on U.S. soil. As soon as the Beatles had had their initial record success in early 1963, they had knocked on the American door. Capitol had turned them down, but other U.S. companies were interested. One of these, Vee Jay Records, a Chicago company, seeing the excitement in Britain decided to take a chance on the Beatles and issued their first American release, "Please Please Me" / "Ask Me Why," in February 1963. They followed with "From Me to You" / "Thank You Girl" in May. Even though neither release raised any excitement with U.S. audiences, the plucky Vee Jay, still eyeing the Beatles' incredible British success, released the boys' first U.S. album, *Introducing the Beatles*, in July. Identical to the Beatles' smash British album *Please Please Me*, it caused hardly a ripple on the American landscape. Of course Vee Jay was a small company with limited promotional funds. In the fall of 1963, the Beatles had remained virtually unheard of in the United States.

It wasn't until the end of 1963 that Capitol finally opened up eyes and ears, and in the face of what was now a true phenomenon, agreed to release a Beatles record. The first Capitol release was "I Saw Her Standing There" / "I Want to Hold Your Hand." There were probably several reasons why Capitol suddenly figured out that the golden goose was at their fingertips. One was that the demand for Beatles' records was suddenly rampant in the United States. Some of their British hits had been brought into the country, and disc jockeys, seeing what was going on in Britain and on the continent, had started playing them. Beatlemania was spreading like a brushfire, and record stores were besieged by wild-eyed fans. Another reason rang out of a headline that appeared in a December issue of *Cash Box*, the record trade magazine: THE BEATLES ARE COMING![5] A personal appearance by the Beatles would help promote the record.

Brian had been interested in getting the Beatles to the United States since midsummer of 1963. Probably the dream had been there even earlier, but it was during that summer that an American promoter, Sid Bernstein, approached Brian with an offer to book the Beatles into New York's Carnegie Hall, one of the great U.S. concert halls. Brian's eyes grew wide, especially at the mention of the fee of close to $7,000 for two shows, considerably more than they were getting in England. But Brian, whose business sense was uncanny, thought the time was not yet ripe for the Beatles in America.

They really had no name recognition in the United States then, and their initial sales there had been dismal. That fall, Brian got together again with Bernstein, this time in New York City. Things were looking better for a U.S. visit, and Brian agreed to the concert, on the condition he could back out if the Beatles did not have a hit U.S. record by the end of the year. The date for Carnegie Hall was set for February 12, 1964.

While in New York, Brian scored another even greater booking coup that would spread the Beatles' fame farther and wider than ever before: he signed them onto the *Ed Sullivan Show*. At that time, the *Ed Sullivan Show* was the most widely watched television variety show in the United States and probably the world. Ed Sullivan had been at Heathrow Airport in London several months earlier at the same time as the Beatles were there and had witnessed what had become a common Beatles airport phenomenon. Of course he was interested in any group that could draw such a huge and wildly enthusiastic crowd, even if he had never heard of them or knew their music. So when Brian went to see the great impresario, little salesmanship was required.

Sullivan offered the Beatles his usual performance fee, which of course was top dollar, but he did not offer them top billing. Much to Sullivan's amazement, Brian would not settle for less than top billing. British acts never got top billing. Finally, they struck a deal. The Beatles would take less money, almost half the usual fee, for two live shows and one taped show, but they would take top billing. The dates were set for February 9 and 16, and a taped session to be shown February 23.

Sullivan did not know it then, but he had just swung the best deal of his life. By the time the Beatles hit the U.S. shores, Beatlemania was raging throughout the land.

FOURTEEN

THE BEATLES CONQUER THE U.S.A.

Barbara Nicholson, 17, of West Hempstead, L.I. said: "I couldn't stand Elvis Presley, I hated Fabian, but I see those guys and I go out of my mind."
—New York Times, Feb. 8, 1964, by Nora Ephron

The only thing that's different is the hair, as far as I can see. I give them a year.
—Ray Block, *Ed Sullivan Show* musical director, quoted in the New York Times, Feb. 8, 1964

Just as Britain was ripe for the merriment of the Beatles after the Profumo scandal, so the United States was ready for a distraction after its horrendous tragedy, the assassination of President John F. Kennedy in November 1963. From shortly after Kennedy's death to when the Beatles arrived in the country, Beatlemania built to a fever pitch in America. It was as though the Beatles had come as a balm to heal the nation's deeply wounded psyche, to divert the people from their sorrow. One writer a decade later said that in the postassassination period, "the Beatles became a safety valve for the release of trauma-wrought tensions."[1] This is just one theory of why Beatlemania caught on with a vengeance in the United States.

There were others. Some said that it was all generated from the hype created by the megapublicity campaign that Capitol Records initiated after they finally realized what they had. Sociologists, psychologists, and psychiatrists had a field day after the Beatles' arrival. Beatlemania was caused by adolescent revolt; peer status from being a Beatlemaniac; sex appeal derived from their erotic music and their stage antics; their boyish appeal to the mother instinct of girls and women; their status as working-class lads who made good and forced the upper class to pay homage to them; their long hair that gave them kind of a dual sexuality.[2] The analyses went on and on. But years, even decades, later, most experts would point to one root cause of Beatlemania: they played great music and could charm your socks off. There wasn't anything around that could compare to them. They were originals.

After the Beatles broke the rock/pop barrier in the United States, a whole host of British stars flooded the American market. Now British groups were in tremendous demand. The Monkees, the Animals, Cream, the Rolling Stones, to name a few, all spun off the Beatles and one way or the other imitated the Beatles' act.

Before the Beatles came to the United States, they had a second appearance at the Palladium and then on January 14 flew to Paris for a three-week booking at the Olympia Theater beginning January 16. It turned out to be one of the very few decisions Brian made for the Beatles that went a bit awry. Paris, it turned out, wasn't quite ready to jump on the Beatlemania bandwagon. The group's opening night was a particular downer when, before a packed house in formal dress, the microphones failed several times, leaving both the boys and the audience disgruntled.

It wasn't that they did not perform well in Paris, it was just that they were not the sensation there that they were everywhere else. Although their spirits were slightly deflated because of their lack of impact on the French market, they were suddenly uplifted by the arrival of a telegram. They could scarcely believe the news: because of the tremendous demand, "I Want to Hold Your Hand" had been released early in the United States, on December 26, 1963, and had shot up to number one on the charts in about two weeks. It was said to be selling at the rate of 10,000 records an hour in New York City alone.

This is just what Brian was hoping would happen prior to the U.S. trip. The Paris experience notwithstanding, the boys were overjoyed and raring to take on America. The staid and proper Brian was so delighted that he allowed himself to be photographed with a chamber pot cocked jauntily on his head.

The Beatles were the first British group to make it to number one on the U.S. charts. Before the Beatles left for the United States, Capitol released its first Beatles album, *Meet the Beatles,* and like the single, it zoomed right to the top, hitting number one on February 15, after the Beatles had already landed. The wild scramble for records did not just benefit Capitol. Vee Jay, the Chicago company that had unsuccessfully released the first Beatle records in the United States when they were unknown, now reaped huge profits. They marketed the recordings they had the rights to in every conceivable form and combination. Meanwhile, Capitol was rushing plans to market everything that EMI, their British parent company, had released to date.

On the crisp afternoon of February 7, 1964, the Beatles, Brian, Cynthia Lennon, several reporters and an entourage of handlers boarded a Pan American jet and began their historic flight to the United States. Heathrow Airport was clogged with thousands of well-wishers who had come to see their idols off, along with the masses of reporters and photographers. As far as most anyone could remember, it was the most momentous send-off ever given anyone leaving British shores.

On the flight across, a matter of about seven-and-a-half hours, the Beatles were somewhat jittery despite the overwhelming success of their records in the United States. George, who unlike the other Beatles, had already visited the United States, expressed his dour thoughts to one of the reporters on the plane: "They've got everything over there," he said. "What do they want us for." And Ringo piped in, "just because we were popular in Britain, why should we be there?"[3]

The Beatles may well have had cause to be fearful of what lay ahead in the United States but not for the reasons they thought. They could only guess at what their reception would be in America. As the plane taxied in, they began to get the idea: thousands and thousands of fans lining the observation decks and waiting areas; hundreds of reporters and dignitaries lining the arrival area. In fact, the airport was so jammed, the din so great, that they briefly thought someone else, the president perhaps, was arriving. The London airport scenes were diminished by this astonishing display. The Beatles need not have feared indifference in the United States; the possibility of being crushed by adoring fans, however, was a real threat.

The press conference that took place at the airport stands as a classic in journalism. Here are some of the questions and answers:

Q.   WILL YOU SING FOR US?
JOHN: WE NEED MONEY FIRST. (APPLAUSE).
Q.   DO YOU HOPE TO GET HAIRCUTS.
JOHN: WE HAD ONE YESTERDAY.
Q.   WHAT DO YOU THINK OF BEETHOVEN?
RINGO: I LOVE HIM, ESPECIALLY HIS POEMS.
Q.   WHAT ABOUT THE MOVEMENT IN DETROIT TO STAMP
        OUT THE BEATLES?
PAUL: WE'VE GOT A CAMPAIGN OF OUR OWN TO STAMP OUT
        DETROIT.
Q.   DO YOU KNOW YOU'RE KEEPING KIDS OUT OF SCHOOL?
JOHN: THAT'S A DIRTY LIE.

The American press was charmed by the Beatles. The journalists loved that the young Englishmen would not take anything seriously—especially themselves. The boys were down to earth, they were funny, they always said the unexpected, always had an off-the-wall answer for any reporter's questions. They were, in short, a great interview, a reporter's dream. Everything they did or said was news.

After the press conference, the Beatles were whisked off to the swank Plaza Hotel in limousines. As they approached the hotel, the streets were lined with screaming, frenzied teenagers all wanting to glimpse their idols. The fans were held off by a large contingent of New York's finest, both mounted and on foot. It had taken several years in Britain for Beatlemania to achieve the pitch that occurred in only two or three months in the United States. At the Plaza, one of New York's most exclusive and dignified hotels, the staff never knew what hit them. The rooms were all booked under Brian's name, which no one knew, and they were expecting a group of English businessmen, not the notorious Beatles. Young girls tried every way to breech security and get to the Beatles. Some almost made it. One maid reported finding three girls hiding in a Beatle's bathtub.

Although the Plaza staff was initially shocked at the ballyhoo surrounding their guests, they recovered and gave the Beatles the royal treatment. Although the boys had to be very careful in moving about because the teenage admirers kept a round-the-clock vigil outside the hotel, they did manage to enjoy some of the city's nightlife. None other than Murray the K, perhaps New York's most famous disc jockey, escorted them to exclusive restaurants and nightclubs, introducing them to various young stars in the city.

A crisis erupted when George came down with a throat infection after the Beatles had landed in New York, and it looked as though he might miss the *Ed Sullivan Show*, their first televised appearance in the United States. His sister Louise, who lived in America, had come to visit and was able to nurse him, and a doctor was brought in. George missed most of the rehearsal, and it was touch and go right up to performance time on February 9.

One of the largest audiences in television history, a

record-breaking 73 million viewers, were not disappointed; George, in the finest show-business tradition, was there for the curtain. It was as though the whole country had been waiting breathlessly for this one moment. Curiosity about seeing and hearing the Beatles in their first U.S. visit had turned the entertainment world upside down, and the desire to witness this phenomenon live on television was intense. People everywhere were rearranging their lives so that they would be free and in front of their sets when the *Ed Sullivan Show* came on. It was even rumored that the Beatles had tempted Billy Graham, the famous evangelist, to break his vow never to watch television on the Sabbath.

Finally the moment arrived. The Beatles were scheduled to open the show and then come back at the end and close the show. It turned out to be the worst possible format for the other acts. Of course, the theater was filled with teenagers who screamed from the time the Beatles were introduced until they played their last note to end the show. The unfortunate performers who came on between the Beatles' appearances never had a chance. For some, their chance for fame was obliterated by the screaming, which hardly subsided between the Beatles' numbers.

During their opening act, they sang "All My Loving," "Till There Was You," and "She Loves You." At the end of the show, they sang "I Saw Her Standing There" before ending with their runaway smash hit, "I Want to Hold Your Hand." Philip Norman called their appearance a "moment simultaneously gratifying America's need for a new idol, a new toy, a painkilling drug and a laugh."[4]

Two days after the first *Ed Sullivan Show*, the boys were scheduled to play the coliseum in Washington, D.C. Brian booked them onto a local flight, but the day of their departure New York City was struck by a snowstorm, and the Beatles (probably recalling Buddy Holly's fate under similar conditions) to a man refused to board the plane. Hasty arrangements were made for rail accommodations. On extremely short notice, a private railcar was arranged for and the boys pulled out in time to make the concert. Word got out that they were now traveling by train and the fans, of course, jammed the stations at both ends.

On the evening of February 11, the Beatles stepped on the coliseum stage and performed their first U.S. concert. In most respects it was like their other concerts—the screaming, the crying, the fainting, the pandemonium—only more so. The coliseum was probably the largest house the Beatles had ever played. It was usually a sports arena and could hold up to 20,000, and it was jammed that night. Moreover, the stage was at the center of the arena, surrounded on all sides by an inclined seating area. This was a new arrangement for the boys, as was the stage itself, which rotated as they played.

With that many people screaming in an enclosed area, the boys could not hear themselves play, but play they did, and the audience loved them. An additional complication hampered their performance: the jelly-babies story had reached the United States, and the American fans took to throwing them at the band just as the British fans had. The only difference was that British jelly babies are soft and American jellybeans are hard. On the revolving stage the candy came at them from all angles, sometimes whole packages at a time. "It was terrible," George said. "They hurt . . . like bullets."[5] Nevertheless, the boys were exhilarated by the success of their first U.S. concert, which was filmed for later showing on closed-circuit television.

Thousands of fans crowded the station in New York waiting for them to return the next day but were disappointed because the Beatles' private railcar was sidetracked before the train pulled into the station. The band escaped back to the hotel without incident, although the *New York Times* reported that "wild-eyed mobs" pursued their idols at the Plaza and elsewhere in near-hysteria. The Beatles barely had a chance to take a breath before being whisked to the first of the two Carnegie Hall concerts that were booked for that evening. It was the same scene inside and outside the hall as the Beatles had experienced everywhere else. A reporter from one journal wrote, "Screaming girls everywhere. . . . They were leaping about in ecstacy and leaning way over the balconies. At any moment I expected to see a body plunge down. . . . Parents looked at their off-spring in bewilderment and the cops looked nervous."[6] The *New York Times* review the next day reported, "Twenty-nine hundred ecstatic Beatlemaniacs gave a concert last night at Carnegie Hall accompanied by the thumping, twanging rhythms of the Beatles."

The next stop was Miami, where the Beatles would appear on their second *Ed Sullivan Show*. While in New York the Beatles had received another important gauge of their success in America: their two Capitol releases, "I Want to Hold Your Hand" and the LP *Meet the Beatles* were officially verified as the fastest-selling records in American record-industry history. Elated over this latest triumph, the Beatles took off for Miami, where they encountered another airport scene of thousands of shrieking fans and the usual mobs of media people. They managed to make it into their waiting limousines safely, but the throbbing, exuberant, teenage crowd left in their wake a shattered plate glass door and windows and some damaged automobiles.

Their second *Ed Sullivan Show* appearance, on February 16, which was broadcast from the Deauville Hotel, was also a record breaker, topping the first show. The Beatles had been scheduled to return the next day to New York, but needing a break and falling prey to the warm, seductive Florida breezes they stayed on until the following Friday, enjoying the ambience of a Capitol executive's seaside mansion. They flew back to New York at the end of the week and returned to London on February 21, besotted with the enormity of their U.S. conquest.

Now they set their sights on the rest of the world.

FIFTEEN

WORLD CONQUEST

A Hard Day's Night was, in essence, a fantasy version of the Beatles' fantasy life that nevertheless conveyed a sense of how Beatlemania looked and felt from the inside.

—Mark Hertsgaard, *A Day in the Life*

B rian Epstein had an agenda for the boys to follow in their conquest of the rest of the world. But first there was other business—the movie business. United Artists had approached the group in late 1963 with a deal for making motion pictures, and they had accepted. Shooting began on March 2, 1964, and continued until late April. United Artists was not looking for a high-budget film, nor did they have great expectations for a large gross on the production. What they saw as the real moneymaker was the musical sound tracks that they would garner from each film. The movie company felt the Beatles' popularity would pull the film through, and the company would make tons on the sound-track recordings.

To direct the film they chose an American, Richard Lester, who had been working in Britain. He had a few credentials in feature filmmaking and had also directed television commercials. The writer was Alun Owen, a Welshman recognized for his television dramas. The film that emerged was essentially a reflection of the everyday life of the Beatles at the height of their popularity. Scenes depict them fleeing pursuing masses of young girls, making harrowing escapes, playing in front of hysterical audiences, trapped in hotel rooms, and showcasing their Liverpudlian wit and charm. The boys played themselves, so in a sense, did not really have to learn to act.

The film turned out to be a success, both financially and artistically, beyond almost anyone's expectations. Shot in black and white, it was nominated for two Academy Awards, including one for screenwriting. It was an international hit. In the United States it opened at 500 theaters simultaneously on the day after its New York premier on August 13, 1964. It drew excellent reviews from even the toughest critics in the *New York Times* and the London *Times*. The *Los Angeles Times* reviewer and other critics even compared the Beatles to the Marx Brothers.

Perhaps the most important, and probably the most enduring, aspect of the film is its music. All the songs were composed by John and Paul, and the subsequent album became their first to be composed of all original Beatles music. It consisted of thirteen tracks, seven of which, including the title song, were from the movie; the others were composed for the album. The American version, however, contained only the music from the movie. Of course, both versions went right to the top of the charts.

The name of the movie and title song is generally attributed to an offhanded comment Ringo made after a long day of filming, which did not finish until nightfall. It was nearing the end of the shoot and a title was desperately needed for the movie. John grabbed Ringo's remark—that it had been a hard day's night—and wrote *A Hard Day's Night* overnight, giving the movie both its title and title song. According to Mark Hertsgaard, the music for *A Hard Day's Night* marked the first sign of a turning point in the Beatles' style, however subtle. Some of the aspects of later works were introduced here: different themes, the fading in and out of tracks, orchestral instrumentation, and the beginnings of more melodic, ballad-style mood pieces, such as Paul's "And I Love Her."[1]

A Hard Day's Night was the first chance for most people to see what the Beatles were really like. The plan was for the boys to be the same on-screen as they were off. Their carefree, irreverent attitude and their sense of humor came through in the movie, just as it did in real life. But most importantly, they had fun with their parts, and their fun spread to the audience.

During the shooting of the film, the Beatles' popularity continued to increase, although they played no gigs during that period. Record sales grew at an incredible rate. In the United States at the beginning of March their singles held the top five positions on the *Billboard* charts, and seven other positions as well. The top five were: 1. "Can't Buy Me Love," 2. "Twist and Shout," 3. "She Loves You," 4. "I Want to Hold Your Hand," 5. "Please Please Me." Their two U.S. albums held the number one and two spots for LPs. No one before or since has so totally dominated the record charts.

Other important nonmusical events were taking place in their lives as well. One of these was a direct result of making the film. During the shoot George met Pattie Boyd, who would become his wife. Pattie had worked in television commercials directed by Richard Lester, who cast her as one of the teenage girls in the movie. George and Pattie's romance took off quickly, and she went to live with him in his new house in Esher near London. They took their wedding vows in January 1966.

Romance was already blooming in other Beatle lives. Ringo had been involved with Maureen Cox since she was a seventeen-year-old Cavern Club groupie. He had just joined the Beatles, and it was just at that time that the Beatles began their heavy travel schedule. So the courtship was interrupted before it had a chance to really take hold. When Ringo moved to London, it seemed they might be separated for good, but when he went to the hospital with tonsillitis in late 1964, she came to visit. That seemed to seal the relationship. He was twenty-four and Maureen was just eighteen when they became engaged; they married in February 1965.

Papa John was already the old married man by comparison with the others. Paul had quietly begun a relationship in April 1963 with Jane Asher, a young actress whose character reflected her upper-middle-class rearing and education. She and Paul were companions for several years, and although she influenced him and inspired him personally and professionally, they never married.

Amazingly, despite moviemaking, songwriting, recording, and fatherhood, John managed to squeeze yet another activity into his life. He had always had a passion to write and draw, and in late March 1964 his first book, *In His Own Write*, was published. It comprised a collection of John's writings and drawings, virtually all of which is purely fanciful. His writing is an almost continuous play on words, as is the title, and the drawings are often cartoonlike and surreal. There was a lot of skepticism when the book first came out. Many people thought John was just taking advantage of his popularity by publishing a book, and of course, anything with his name on it would sell. But the Beatles always seemed to exceed expectations, and John's literary effort was no exception. He was guest of honor at a Foyle's Literary Lunch, and a *Times Literary Supplement* reviewer quoted by Hunter Davies said, "It is worth the attention of anyone who fears for the impoverishment of the English language and the British imagination."

Also during March, the Beatles' images were enshrined in Madame Tussaud's Wax Museum, and in April their next album, *The Beatles Second Album*, was released in the United States. (It was Capitol's second Beatles album release.)

With filming finally completed at the end of April, the boys looked forward to their first world tour, scheduled to begin June 4, 1964. It would take them to several European countries, and for the first time they would press on to Asian and Pacific ports, including Hong Kong, Australia, and New Zealand. Riding atop a wave of unprecedented world popularity, they were preparing to depart, when there was a sudden and quite frightening disruption. Ringo collapsed the day before their embarkation date and was rushed to the hospital. He was suffering from a severe case of tonsillitis, and the doctor ordered him hospitalized for at least several days.

Panic ensued. There was some talk of canceling until Ringo recovered, but that was dismissed. They had to find a quality substitute drummer immediately who could leave on twenty-four-hours notice. The first name that came up was Jimmy Nicol, a drummer who had performed Beatles material on an LP called *Beatlemania*. A desperate call was put through. The next day Jimmy Nicol was on a plane with the other three Beatles headed for the first stop on their world tour, Copenhagen, Denmark.

From Denmark, the Beatles went to the Netherlands, their last European stop before heading for Hong Kong. They arrived in the British colony on June 9, and the reception was the same as in Europe and America despite the greater distance and cultural differences. Hong Kong is a shopper's paradise, but the Beatles were confined to the theater and their hotel rooms because of the danger of being crushed by their frantic fans. There were heavy police escorts, but the crowd pressure was too great to guarantee safety. The only way they could shop was to have the merchants come to the hotel, which they did in a steady stream, displaying their wares of clothing, jewelry, cameras, and the like.

The greetings and the crowd scenes were the same in Australia and New Zealand, and the jelly babies continued to rain down on them everywhere. It is estimated that the crowd sizes in Australia broke all existing records. In Adelaide alone about 300,000 bodies packed the streets to welcome the Fab Four. Apparently, the absence of Ringo had not diminished their appeal a single wit. Accompanied by Brian, Ringo finally caught up with the others in Melbourne, Australia, and reclaimed his drummer's chair from

Jimmy Nicol on June 15. After New Zealand the boys returned to Australia for a booking in Brisbane before returning to London. Despite their incredible popularity in
Australia, the Beatles never returned there.

The Beatles' return to England was fairly brief, as their
next major tour, back to America, was already set for mid-
August. The highlight of their stay was the premiere of *A
Hard Day's Night* in London. Princess Margaret and Lord
Snowdon were in attendance, and the royal couple also
graced an exclusive party attended by the boys afterward,
an honor afforded to few. But possibly more meaningful for
them was the opening of the movie in Liverpool, where it
seemed the whole town turned out to welcome its returning heroes. At the official town-hall ceremony, a local dig-
nitary told the crowd that Liverpool gave the Beatles to the
world. John was then heard to comment, "And the world
has lobbed us back at Liverpool."[2]

The movie sound-track recording was released about
the same time along with the single of the title song. Both
climbed immediately to the top of the charts in Britain, the
United States, and elsewhere.

And then on August 18 the Beatles boarded a plane
bound for San Francisco, the initial stop of their first North
American tour. This would be the most ambitious and
strenuous tour ever attempted by the Beatles and probably
drained them of any love they may have had for touring.
In slightly more than one month, they were scheduled to
perform thirty-two shows in twenty cities. But this was not
Britain where cities are only a few hours apart. This was
the vast expanse of North America, and the Beatles logged
almost 25,000 miles to make all their dates. They were in
the air for almost sixty hours.[3]

The tour was a nightmare of logistics that took the Beatles American agent, Norman Weiss, six months to plan. He
likened it to planning the invasion of Normandy. It was
probably something they wished they had not attempted
on such a grand scale, although the trip netted them an-

other huge paycheck. But as huge as it was they could have made much more; they were so popular they could have charged almost any ticket price they chose and still filled every house they played.

To Brian's credit, however, and to the Beatles' as well, they would not allow the local impresarios to gouge the fans. Anyone who has bought tickets to a rock concert in the 1990s knows how rare such concerns have become. Norman Weiss would say that Brian wanted to be fair to the fans. "We had it written into all the contracts, stating what the prices had to be. . . . Every promoter agreed, thankful to be putting them [the Beatles]on."4

But while the Beatles were being thoughtful to their fans—they were making money at a bewildering rate anyway—there was greed and scheming all around them. Probably one of the most bizarre get-rich-off-the-Beatles schemes was hatched by some money-hungry Chicago entrepreneurs who bought the sheets and pillowcases the Beatles slept on, cut them into thousands of small squares, labeled them with the appropriate Beatle name, and sold them for a small amount each. In the midst of Beatlemania, the fans were ready to pay dearly for anything that smacked of Beatles, but somehow this scam lacked appeal and the investors reportedly did poorly. Quite literally people tried to make everything the Beatles touched turn into gold.

By the time the Beatles wrapped up their first North American tour they had played virtually all of the major venues in the United States and Canada, including the Cow Palace in San Francisco, the Empire Stadium in Vancouver, the Hollywood Bowl in Los Angeles, the International Amphitheater in Chicago, Olympia Stadium in Detroit, Maple Leaf Gardens in Toronto, the Forum in Montreal, the Boston Garden, Municipal Stadium in Kansas City, and Memorial Auditorium in Dallas.

The tour ended on a high note at the Paramount Theater in New York City. It was a sold-out concert benefitting cerebral palsy and retarded infant charities. People paid up to $100 a ticket to see the Beatles and other celebrities, resulting in a benefit to the charities of some $25,000. The Beatles were presented with a plaque thanking them for bringing "hope and help to the handicapped children of America." A few hours later an exhausted Beatles entourage was over the Atlantic winging homeward, on top of the world as no one had ever been before.

BEATLEMANIA FOREVER

Beatles concerts are nothing to do with music anymore. They're just bloody tribal rites.

—John Lennon, from *The Beatles Live*
by Mark Lewisohn

We got in a rut, going round the world. Nobody could hear. It was just a bloody big row. We got worse as musicians. There was no satisfaction at all.

—George Harrison, from *The Beatles:
The Authorized Biography* by Hunter Davies

The Beatles were growing weary. So was Brian. So were the managers and handlers and everyone else connected with the tours. Never again would they attempt anything as arduous as their first North American tour. Back home the boys rested for a little more than two weeks before embarking on a tour of the United Kingdom. It was almost as long as the U.S. tour, but they were home and the strain was not so great as foreign touring. Still, they had to cope with the bedlam of Beatlemania, still going full blast in Britain. And being at home, they were also squeezing recording dates in with the tour schedule.

How long could they keep it up? By the end of 1964, the grind of touring was becoming an increasingly pressing problem. It is difficult enough for well-known personalities to move about, being hounded by fans and media and having their personal lives exposed on a daily basis. But for the

Beatles it was all of this multiplied many times over. At this point in their careers they were in almost daily threat of bodily harm. They needed bodyguards and police escorts everywhere they went. They were literally prisoners in their hotel rooms, in their homes, in the studio, wherever they went. They were not free to come and go as they pleased, and the need to break out was becoming intense.

It had been about a year since the Beatles had cut their first record, and they were already millionaires. They would all become millionaires many times over. Their fees for performances were now the highest anyone could demand. But earning such huge amounts of money was becoming meaningless. Hunter Davies wrote in their biography, "Being rich and powerful enough to enter any door was pointless. They were trapped."[1]

Not that there wasn't still excitement. They still got a charge out of being the "toppermost of the poppermost," the most popular entertainers in the world and producers of the hottest selling discs of all time. But everyone has his breaking point. The Beatles hadn't quite reached it by the end of 1964, but the seams were starting to come apart. They fondly recalled sweating and toiling eight hours a day in Hamburg and enjoying every minute. On tour now they worked usually no more than about an hour a day, but it was hardly fun.

The Beatles still had commitments to meet, however, and the boys would honor them. Their next junket, scheduled for April 1965, would kick off in France, followed by engagements in Italy and Spain. This would be a quick two-week jaunt, and then in August they would be off on their second North American tour, which would also be held to about two weeks.

They were hardly idle in the intervening months between the end of their U.K. tour in November 1964 and their European trip. First they cut another album, *Beatles for Sale* (*Beatles '65* in the United States), which was released in December. This quickly hit the top as did anything with the

Beatles stamp at that time, but it was not that well received critically. The Beatles were exhausted from their U.S. excursion and had only time to put eight new tunes together for the album, the remaining six being standards from the Cavern Club period. The combination of the time crunch and their physical and mental weariness seemed to take its toll in the album's quality.

The best tracks on the album, according to Beatles musicologist Mark Hertsgaard, are "No Reply," "I'm a Loser," and "Eight Days a Week." The non-Beatle fare included "Rock and Roll Music," "Kansas City," and "Mr. Moonlight." The album, if not highly regarded, at least represented for John Lennon the first indication of a new direction in his songwriting. He called it "my Dylan period," referring to the influence of folk-rock artist Bob Dylan, whom they had met in the United States and who had been gathering a huge following with his socially significant lyrics. Similarly, John's work became "more realistic, introspective, and diverse." It also included, in "She's a Woman," what was probably the first reference to the Beatles' use of marijuana, also ascribed to Dylan's influence.[2]

At the beginning of December, Ringo finally had his tonsillectomy, and to no one's surprise numerous requests came from fans who wanted the tonsils. Although collectors were willing to pay dearly for them, Ringo would not consider any offers, and the organs were destroyed. Later in the month and into January, the Beatles were featured in a Christmas show—something they did for several years running—and then it was back to moviemaking. Their second film was set to begin shooting in February following a brief holiday.

Help!, as the new film was to be called, stood in sharp contrast to *A Hard Day's Night*. Both films were produced in less than three months, but *Help!* cost more than twice as much to make. It was shot in color, and unlike the first film, it had a semblance of plot. The boys again played themselves, but they were woven into the story, with

Ringo playing a key role. The story revolves around a ring possessed by Ringo, which happens to be the missing sacred relic of an Eastern cult, the members of which are desperate to regain possession of the item. A number of harrowing escapes ensue.

Help! was not nearly as well received critically as the foursome's first movie. It lacked some of the charm, wit, and artistic quality of *A Hard Day's Night*, but, as with the first film, fans came to see it in droves, and it was a box-office success. The one way in which the two movies were artistically close was in the music. Again the title song was composed by John, and while at the time nobody recognized it as such, "Help!" has been interpreted as a personal reflection of John's mental framework at the time. It was a kind of crying out against what was happening to him and the other Beatles in their rapid-paced, nonstop lives. The lyrics reveal his mood:

> *Help me if you can, I'm feeling down*
> *And I do appreciate your being 'round*
> *Help me get my feet back on the ground,*
> *won't you please help me?*

The other songs written new for *Help!* included, by John and Paul, "Ticket to Ride," "You're Going to Lose That Girl," "The Night Before," "You've Got to Hide Your Love Away," and, by George, "I Need You." All of these appeared on the sound-track album along with several other compositions. The album became another number-one hit in Britain and the United States, as did a number of singles from the album.

Two other striking events took place in the first half of 1965. One of these was an honor the Beatles never dreamed would be bestowed on them and which provoked intense controversy in the United Kingdom. On June 12, word came from Buckingham Palace that the kingdom's prestigious Member of the Order of the British Empire

(MBE) award would be conferred upon the Beatles. This award is usually bestowed upon military or civilian personnel for their meritorious service to the country. To many, it seemed that giving such an award to rock stars was debasing the honor associated with the award. A number of awardees even returned their medals in protest.

On the other side of the controversy there was also a large contingent—including Prime Minister Harold Wilson, who had recommended the Beatles in the first place—who felt the honor was deserved. The Beatles' value to Britain went beyond their music. As George put it, "I didn't think you got that sort of thing, just for playing rock 'n' roll music."[3] Obviously, the Beatles were also an economic asset and had been called Britain's greatest export. They had opened the floodgates of British pop music to the world and raised the stature of British pop artists everywhere. That effect has continued to the present day.

Except for John, the Beatles had no problem accepting the medals. Despite being a millionaire, John remained an anti-establishment, blue-collar lad and was ready to turn it down because he thought it was phony royal puffery. But Brian talked him into accepting, because it would hurt the group if he refused. Years later he returned the medal in protest over British policies in Africa and Vietnam.

Shortly after the award announcement, John published his second book, *A Spaniard in the Works*. It did not receive quite the notices of the first book, but in combination with the earlier work, it was adopted for stage presentation in 1968.

The Beatles left for their European tour at the end of June 1965. Interestingly, for the first time in years, not all of the Beatles' concerts were sold out. There may have been several reasons for this, other than waning popularity. One was that it was an exceedingly hot summer, especially in Italy, where some of the shows were booked into sweltering indoor venues. Another is that the European fans may have just begun to question paying a heavy ticket price to go to a twenty-five-minute performance where you couldn't hear the music.

The U.S tour that followed began in August. Maybe the heat wasn't as bad, and maybe the fans were more foolish, but in America Beatlemania, if anything, had picked up more steam. The trip was shorter than the first one, but more fans would actually get to see them. This was because on this trip the Beatles would play only in the largest outdoor stadiums of the cities on the tour.

The crowning glory of the whole tour, if not their entire performance career, was the opening concert in New York City. They were booked into Shea Stadium, where the New York Mets play baseball. There, even the jaded Beatles were exhilarated by the size and intensity of the crowd, and they put on an inspired performance that was recorded on film for a television presentation. Fifty-five thousand fans jammed the stadium, paying a total of more than $300,000 for their seats. It was the largest audience and the largest gross at that point in entertainment history.[4]

Getting to and from the stadium was the usual military operation. This time they traveled by limousine to a heliport and took a helicopter to a point close to the stadium, where a waiting armored car took them to the ballpark. Hundreds of police and security guards were assigned to keep order while the Beatles played, but the band could not be heard above the screaming, sobbing, fainting audience.

The rest of the tour went the same way, but the Beatles were now highly contemptuous of what for them had become a circus that lacked redeeming value and had nothing to do with their musicianship. They were, at least, largely relieved of the pressure of airport mob scenes by landing in remote airstrips, not caring if their fans even caught a glimpse of them, safety and sanity having become the prime concerns.

In Houston this didn't work. Landing at 2:00 A.M., the Beatles' plane was compelled to use a regular runway.

Thousands of fans broke loose and besieged the Beatles' aircraft. The boys were trapped inside and began to fear for their lives. Fans were swarming all over the plane. The boys were finally rescued by a service truck that they entered from an emergency exit above the crowd.[5]

The riots at the Houston airport were among the most violent of the tour, but there were similar incidents along the way as they completed their schedule with performances in other major venues, including Comiskey Park in Chicago, Metropolitan Stadium in Minneapolis, the Hollywood Bowl in Los Angeles, and the Cow Palace in San Francisco. While in the Los Angeles area, the Beatles fulfilled a kind of dream when they met their idol, the King, Elvis Presley.

The Beatles made more money on the tour than ever before, but enough was enough. They had discussed it with Brian before, but now it was serious: touring must end. The very thought must have depressed Brian, whose whole life was built around the Beatle phenomenon. But even Brian was wearying of the fray, and he must have realized that they could not go on as they had, that it must end before they all went barmy. No one knew then that almost one year from that point they would be playing their last live concert.

NEW SOUNDS, MYSTICISM, AND PSYCHEDELIA

Picture yourself in a boat on a river with tangerine trees and marmalade skies.

—From "Lucy in the Sky with Diamonds"
(Lennon-McCartney)

B ack home, Brian was rubbing his hands over the upcoming fall events for the Beatles. Another royal command performance, another Christmas show, a tour of Britain, the MBE award ceremony, and studio sessions. He was in for a jolt. The Beatles nixed everything except studio work, the MBE ceremony, and an abbreviated tour of Britain. The grind of public appearances had taken its toll, and although the Beatles with their working-class backgrounds and Liverpool roots appreciated all that had come to them, they simply couldn't hack it anymore. They yearned to move about freely, and above all they wanted to get back to their music, which was lost on concert tours.

The minitour of Britain launched in December 1965 took only ten days and played in nine cities. When they finished the final date in Cardiff, Wales, it ended their touring in the United Kingdom. The Beatles would not appear as a group in public again until May 1966. They were one of the groups that performed at a ceremony held in Wembley honoring the *New Musical Express* magazine poll winners. Then it was late June before they would begin what would be their last world tour. The first stop was West Germany. This part of the tour turned out to be nostalgic for the Beatles. One of the cities they played was Hamburg, where they had perfected their rock style. It was also a place where they had grown up socially. There was a warm reunion with old friends who had been there with them through tough but adventurous, fun-filled times. Among them were Astrid Kirchherr, Bert Kaempfert, and a host of other old Reeperbahn buddies. The boys did not forget those who helped them become the Beatles.

From Germany they went directly to Tokyo for their first and only visit. There they saw the beginning of trouble that hounded them through the tour. At first the Beatles were impressed with the tremendous security afforded by the Tokyo government. They had never seen so many police and such outstanding crowd control. They were to learn, however, that this was partly because of trouble from anti-Beatles protest groups.

Some protested that the Beatles' performance was being held in a hall that they considered sacred because of the highly traditional martial arts contests held there. A rock 'n' roll group, they felt, would defile the hall. Others protested on moral grounds, claiming that the Beatles were a corrupting influence on the young. Despite the protests, the Beatles played to a sellout crowd for every one of their five performances. In fact the ticket demand was so great that the Japanese held a lottery for the tickets. *Variety* magazine reported that on opening night, the Beatles, who "came from virtual imprisonment at the Tokyo Hilton," were greeted by a "predominately teenage girl audience [who] screamed, stomped, convulsed, tore hair, and reluctantly held their seats under close police surveillance."[1]

From Tokyo the Beatles flew to Manila, in the Philippines, where they were scheduled for two performances. In the whole history of the Beatles it is doubtful that anything went so outrageously wrong as their Manila visit. It was likely all a matter of miscommunication and misunderstanding, but the Philippines administration was unforgiving. From the moment they got off the plane there were disagreements between Brian and the promoter. Worst of all, the Beatles failed to show up for a reception given for them by the country's first lady, Imelda Marcos, and her daughters. No one in the Beatles' party knew about the 11:00 A.M. date (so they claimed), but no matter, it was regarded by the host country as a deliberate snub, and no explanations or apologies were acceptable.

The repercussions from the incident were dire indeed. There were death threats, receipts from the two concerts the Beatles gave there were withheld, and Brian was forced to pay taxes to the government before they could leave. Their departure was also delayed on the grounds that some of their crew were illegal aliens. Worst of all the government withdrew all security for the Beatles, leaving them and their entourage to make it to the airport on their own. On the way to their departing flight they were jostled and roughed up by angry locals incited by slanted press reports. In the fracas, some of the group, particularly Brian, got hurt. They departed finally, never to return to that country.

On the return trip to England everyone was disgruntled. It was hard to shake off the trauma of the Manila experience. Brian must have seen the handwriting on the wall relative to future touring. There was one more tour already booked, another American jaunt set for August 1966. It turned out this tour, too, would be rife with acrimony. There had always been huge crowds in America, and there had always been a certain amount of danger. But it had always been their overzealous, adoring fans who caused the problems. On this trip, they encountered other problems of a more serious nature, which were largely attributable to a misconstrued statement made by John Lennon.

During an interview the previous year, John, discoursing on religion, told a reporter that Christianity was on the wane and that "We're [the Beatles] more popular than

Jesus now." Many months later, before the next U.S. tour, an American teen magazine reprinted the interview, this time using John's remark out of context in a blazing headline. Of course, in a country where there are many conservative Christian groups, John sounded like the Antichrist coming to America. John's comment in the context of his whole statement was hardly inflammatory, but some people would not consider the whole, and an anti-Beatles movement began to take shape in the United States, especially in the American South, where the so-called Bible belt is noted for its religious conservatism.

The Beatles, in light of other recent experiences on tour, looked askance at the furor going on in the United States. Brian's concern was also great as the media reported protest marches, Ku Klux Klan rallies, bonfires of Beatles records and paraphernalia, and disc jockies denouncing the group and refusing to play their records. Brian even thought of canceling the tour, but at a press conference in Chicago John apologized, and the crisis was defused enough for the tour to go on.[2]

On it went, but not well. Yes, America still loved them—record sales were up and the concerts were still packed—but on several occasions things got out of hand. In Cleveland fans broke through police lines and stormed the stage. There were incidents with the Ku Klux Klan, assassination threats, and even a rain out in Cincinnati, where the stage was left without a canopy. When rain threatened, the boys, hooked up to high-voltage electrical sound systems, were terrified that they would be electrocuted.

Rowdyism may have been partly the cause of empty seats starting to appear in some of the huge U.S. sports stadiums. At the concert in Los Angeles's Dodger Stadium, a near riot broke out. One newspaper reported that "Youths . . . charged the gates with wooden barricades which had been set up to keep the crowds back. . . . They hurled sticks and bottles at police until they were finally turned away. . . . Dozens of people among the 45,000 attending suffered minor injuries." The Beatles themselves escaped in an armored car.[3]

After Los Angeles it was on to San Francisco. The scene was set for the final drama. The place was Candlestick Park, home of the San Francisco Giants, which was always brisk and windy at night. The date was August 29, 1966. That place and time are etched in musical history, for they marked the last real scheduled live concert ever played by the Beatles as a group. After some 1,400 live dates, touring ended.

It was not announced at the time, but everyone knew that it was over. The boys might have been a little sentimental, but largely they were relieved. They knew to some degree where they were going—into the studio to make music. Brian, however, was devastated. He wasn't sure which way to turn because the Beatles' work in the studio and their other projects did not occupy him that much. He had other acts to manage, but the Beatles' tours had been the mainstay of his life. He lived, slept, and ate Beatles. With the tours ended, the dejection was deep and long-lasting.

For the Beatles it was a new beginning, the start of a new chapter. They had gone far and wide on tours, but their musical development, they felt, was just beginning and had a long way to go. Even during their later touring days the music they were writing and recording differed from what they were playing. The live audiences, still mostly teenage girls, demanded the old chart-climbing stuff, "I Want to Hold Your Hand" and the like. It didn't matter much because the audience couldn't hear the music anyway. The newer studio music would have been difficult to present on the stage, especially under the conditions of a typical Beatle concert, because of the introduction of new sounds and the technology required to produce them.

The evolution had been going on through 1965, but in the fall of that year the Beatles produced a groundbreaking album, *Rubber Soul*. There had been hints before of the Beatles using their music as a commentary on the social scene, music that would send a message. "Help!" was one example and another, also from the movie soundtrack album, was "Yesterday," mostly penned by Paul and notable for its drifting melody, unique harmonic structure, and nostalgic theme. So exquisite is "Yesterday" that it went beyond rock to become a standard for pop singers. *Rubber Soul* carried farther their trend toward the use of orchestral instruments and experimentation with studio sound effects.

George Martin would state that *Rubber Soul* was their first album to have an internal unity, unlike earlier ones that more resembled a collection of singles. It included such notable Beatle works as "We Can Work It Out," "Nowhere Man," "Michelle," "In My Life," "Norwegian Wood," and "Girl." The last two of these were the first on which George Harrison would use the sitar, an instrument he learned to play on trips to India. Subsequently he became friends with and took lessons from the internationally renowned Indian sitar player, Ravi Shankar.

Pleased with the results of *Rubber Soul* and seeing that it was well received both artistically and commercially, the Beatles were off and running. Their next studio experience produced *Revolver*, which soared beyond the parameters of *Rubber Soul*. Instrumentation and tonal qualities became more sophisticated even as the compositions sought deeper and more meaningful expression.

This was George's most ambitious album thus far as a composer, with him contributing three pieces to the album. He also continued his work on the sitar, now a trademark sound in Beatles music. *Revolver* has been described as the Beatles' first psychedelic music, a reference to the kind of imagery reportedly brought on by the use of mind-altering drugs. The dreamy, mystic quality of the "Eleanor Rigby" lyric ("wearing the face that she keeps in a jar by the door") typifies the style and mood. The album, another number one on the charts, was regarded as the Beatles' masterpiece to date, and some still think so. Many authorities in the musical world thought that certainly now they had peaked, that they could not surpass this latest work.

There is no consensus on what is the Beatles' greatest musical achievement. Some prefer their earlier, less complicated works. It was their next work, though, that is most often referred to as the crown jewel of the Beatles' musical production. *Sgt. Pepper's Lonely Hearts Club Band* was conceived and produced in the first half of 1967 and released in June of that year. Back in the early days of their touring, the Beatles would rush into the studio and complete an album in about a day. *Sgt. Pepper* took about five months and hundreds of hours of studio time to complete. It was a labor of perfectionism. The Beatles and George Martin tried to make every note count.

Sgt. Pepper was a reflection of everything the Beatles had become up to that point. Their interests, their ideas, their values had been evolving since the end of touring. During the years of touring they had had little time to think; dealing with the day-to-day survival problems was about all they could cope with. Now they had a chance to reflect. They looked about and saw a terrible war in Vietnam, hunger in the world, pollution, the bomb, and other issues confronting the world. They began to look inward, to define themselves as individuals and as a group. They searched for a greater meaning to life. John at one point would cry out, "God, Jesus . . . will you please, just once, tell me what the hell I'm supposed to be doing?"[4] From all of this *Sgt. Pepper's Lonely Hearts Club Band* was born.

The work on *Sgt. Pepper* began in late 1966. The first two songs produced for the album were "Strawberry Fields Forever" and "Penny Lane," both nostalgic portraits of boyhood memories in Liverpool. The two songs never made it onto the album, however. The album was taking so long to produce that the record company insisted on having something to release in the interim. Thus, the first two compositions were released as a single, which is often viewed as the Beatles' finest single despite becoming the first since "Love Me Do" not to be a universal number one. They then plunged into *Sgt. Pepper,* virtually barricading themselves in the studio until the album was completed in late spring 1967.

If *Rubber Soul* and *Revolver* were departures from the Beatles' previous work, *Sgt. Pepper* was a quantum leap into another stratosphere. Now George Martin's creative genius as a record producer was stretched to the limit to create new sounds. Music composed for the album would eventually include the piccolo trumpet; the clarinet; such Indian instruments (George Harrison's influence) as the sitar, the dilruba, the tamboura, the svaramandala, and the table harp; a simulated calliope; a conventional harp; a string octet; and even the forty-one-piece Royal Philharmonic Symphony Orchestra.[5]

The concept of *Sgt. Pepper* alone was groundbreaking. Here they not only created and played the music of a fictional band but became the band itself on the record. On the album cover, arguably the most honored in record-making history, they appear in ornate, military band costumes against a backdrop of sixty-two images of their favorite people, ranging from Albert Einstein to Bob Dylan to Shirley Temple.

The title came from a novel of the same name written by Henry Edwards. It was probably Paul's idea to actually become the band and do the whole album as though it was being recorded by the Sgt. Pepper band. In order to emphasize the thematic quality of the album, the numbers are mostly blended one into the other without a distinct start and stop between them. Although each number has a special quality of its own, the album was designed to be listened to from beginning to end in a single sitting. It even opens with crowd noises and the sound of an orchestra tuning up, just as though a live concert were to begin. Then the group, with orchestral backing, swings into the title song, which sets the tone for the album with heavy bass-drum beats and the oom-pah-pah sound of the marching band. There is even a reprise of the main theme at the end.

Sgt. Pepper continued the psychedelic trend that had begun with *Revolver* and possibly earlier. In fact, the Beatles during this period had been experimenting with mind-altering drugs, such as marijuana and LSD. They had sought to enhance and expand their musical creations by doing so, and several of the songs on the album would seem to speak to or reflect drug use. The Beatles, and particularly John, have denied this, but the connection is not difficult to see.

The songs that appear to have the most obvious links to drug effects include "With a Little Help from My Friends" and "Lucy in the Sky with Diamonds." The latter includes the initials LSD, but John insists it was the title of a drawing made by his son. There is no question the lyric is a poetic fantasy, dreamy and drifting. The BBC long refused to play some of the music of *Sgt. Pepper* because of its suspected drug relatedness.

No matter the source or references of the songs, the album set the musical world on its ear. Other groups trying to imitate or catch up to the Beatles were left in the dust. The songs seem to run the gamut of human conditions and emotions, with beauty and grotesqueness, laughter and tears, and hope and despair permeating the lyrics. For instance "She's Leaving Home" is a poignant story of a daughter separating from her parents, the sadness it creates and the warm memories it evokes. As much as any piece on the album, this contributed to the Beatles becoming the voice of the sixties generation.

The final tune probably makes the strongest statement and arguably had the greatest impact of any Beatles tune. "A Day in the Life" is accompanied by a full orchestra. The main lyric, written and sung by John, is simple but compelling, beginning, "I read the news today, oh boy / About a lucky man who made the grade." Behind the words is a solid drum beat that intensifies emotion and meaning. The lyric continues, "He blew his mind out in a car," "A crowd of people stood and stared," and "The crowd of people turned away / but I just had to look." The bridge, written and sung by Paul, begins "Woke up, fell out of bed / dragged a comb across my head." A sudden switch from

John's poignant, haunting verse. Again, simplicity is blended into a complex musical score.

The piece ends with a full orchestra in a crescendo of ascending cacophony that seems to whirl the simple message into chaos. The last sound is that of three pianos striking the same huge, somber chord simultaneously, creating an ominous, lingering, almost forbidding, tone that reverberates into nothing. John had said he wanted it to end in "a sound like the end of the world," and, with George Martin's technical expertise, he got his wish.[6] No piece of music could have concluded more dramatically.

Sgt. Pepper was released on June 1, 1967, and it was an immediate commercial and almost universal critical success. On the record market it was another Beatles blitz. It sold 250,000 copies in Britain in the first week. In the United States an advance order of more than 1 million preceded sales of 2.5 million in the first three months. Its run on the charts was staggering: 27 weeks on top in Britain, 19 weeks in the States, remaining on the U.S. charts for a total 113 weeks.[7]

The critical accolades were, if anything, even more impressive. Bill Harry, in his encyclopedic work on the Beatles, calls it "Arguably, the most influential album of popular music ever released."[8] In Hertsgaard's work on the Beatles' music, he says that *Sgt. Pepper* "assured the Beatles of their place in history." He quotes the composer Aaron Copland as saying, "If you want to know about the 60s, play the music of the Beatles." Hertsgaard goes on, "Of no album is this more true than *Sgt. Pepper* . . . the album was seen to herald a new era of alternative values, fresh energy, and renewed promise. The critic Kenneth Tynan went so far as to call it 'a decisive moment in the history of western civilization.' " In concluding, Hertsgaard says, "Nothing in popular music was the same after *Sgt. Pepper*."[9]

Some critics saw *Sgt. Pepper* in a lesser light, but most agreed that like the Beatles themselves, the sum was much greater than the individual parts.

LETTING GO AND COMING APART

Why should the Beatles give more? Didn't they give everything on God's earth for ten years? Didn't they give themselves?
—John Lennon, from *Playboy* Magazine interview, January 1980.

After *Sgt. Pepper* the Beatles continued to work together in the studio, but they also followed separate professional and personal paths. George pursued his interest in Eastern philosophy, sparked by his association with Ravi Shankar, and he also began to develop separate musical interests. Both John and Ringo contracted separately for movie roles: John for *How I Won the War*; Ringo for *Candy*. Paul followed separate music interests, took an interest in the Beatles' business dealings, and came to the brink of marriage, going so far as to announce his engagement to Jane Asher. Despite these new interests, their main occupation continued to focus on the things they did as a group. Their next project was to appear on a satellite TV broadcast, the first of its kind, called "Our World." The Beatles, particularly John, were becoming more socially conscious, and the program was designed to promote world unity and brotherhood. It had been several years since the *Ed Sullivan Show*, when they were seen by 73 million viewers. "Our World," presented on June 25, 1967, dwarfed the Sullivan broadcast in audience terms. It reached some 400 million people in twenty-four countries. For the

In November 1963, the Beatles rehearse for the Royal Variety Performance at London's Prince of Wales Theatre. Their appearance at this prestigious event propelled them to superstar status in England.

Fans and photographers line the observation deck and jam the gate area as the Beatles arrive at New York's John F. Kennedy Airport on February 7, 1964. The Beatles were apprehensive about their first U.S. visit, but it turned out to be a colossal success. ♪

The Beatles field questions at a packed press conference soon after arriving in New York. Paul, Ringo, George, and John charmed the press and the public with their wit, charm, and good humor. ♪

A crowd in the grip of Beatlemania shouts, cries, and convulses uncontrollably. Wherever they went, the Beatles were greeted—and often relentlessly pursued—by masses of hysterical fans.

The Beatles perform one of their hits on the Ed Sullivan Show. *Their February 9, 1964, appearance attracted a TV audience of 73 million viewers.*

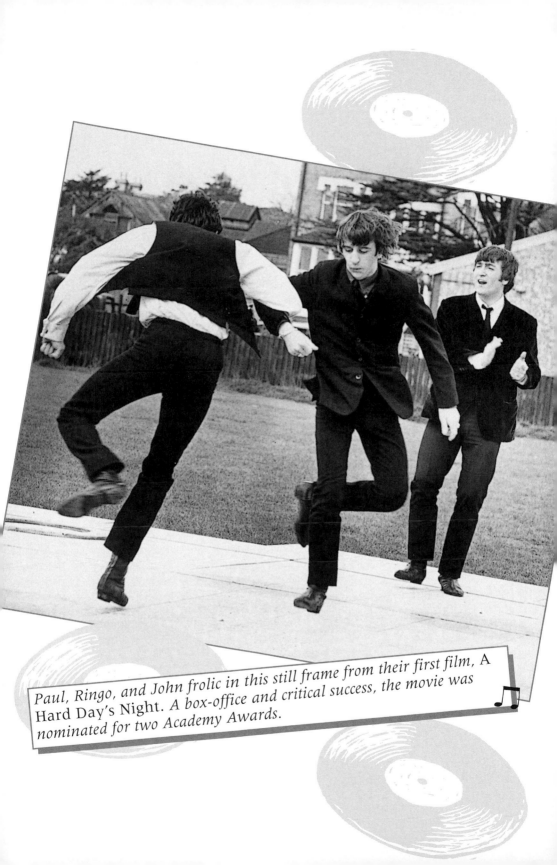

Paul, Ringo, and John frolic in this still frame from their first film, A Hard Day's Night. A box-office and critical success, the movie was nominated for two Academy Awards.

On June 4, 1964, the Beatles embark on their first world tour. Ringo had been hospitalized with a severe case of tonsillitis the previous day, and Jimmy Nicol (holding bag) replaced him for much of the tour.

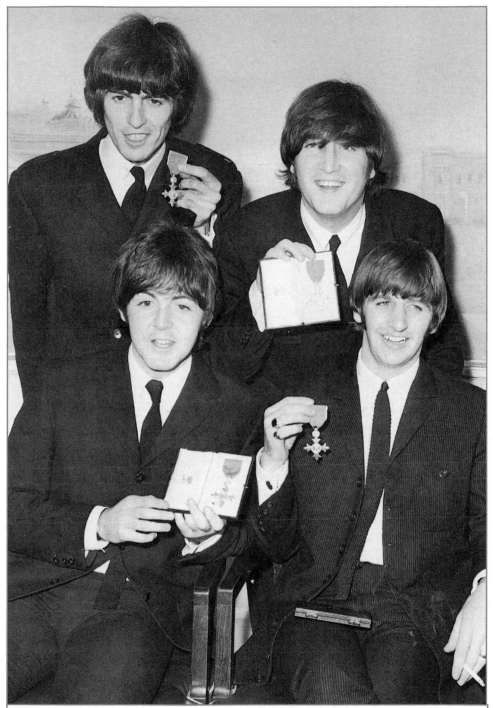

*T*he Beatles show off their prestigious Member of the Order of the British Empire awards, which they received at a Buckingham Palace ceremony on October 16, 1965. Years later, John Lennon would return his medal in protest over British policies in Africa and Vietnam.

On August 15, 1965, the Beatles kicked off their second world tour in New York City. Fifty-five thousand fans packed into Shea Stadium to hear the fabulous foursome.

In August 1966, a group of Jackson, Mississippi, teenagers gather around a bonfire fueled by Beatles records and paraphernalia. An anti-Beatles crusade raged in some parts of the United States when a teen magazine reported that John Lennon had stated the Beatles were "more popular than Jesus now."

On the cover of the Sgt. Pepper's Lonely Hearts Club Band *album*, *the* Beatles appear in front of a backdrop of sixty-two images of their favorite people. Many music scholars, critics, and fans consider Sgt. Pepper *the* most influential pop music album ever recorded.

Paul, George, and John speak with Maharishi Mahesh Yogi. George had introduced his bandmates to the teachings of the guru, who headed a philosophical movement called transcendental meditation.

Yoko Ono and John Lennon pose for a portrait. An American-educated Japanese artist, Ono fueled John's creativity, but her constant presence created tension in the band.

In January 1969, the Beatles play atop London's Twickenham Studios. The rooftop performance was filmed as part of the Let It Be project.

In New York City's Central Park, fans mourn of the death of John Lennon, who was shot by a deranged fan on December 8, 1980. ♪♫

Paul McCartney sings during a Wings concert. ♫

*G*eorge Harrison performs at the Concert for Bangladesh, a benefit show that he organized in 1971. ♪♫

*R*ingo Starr and his All-Starr Band pose for a publicity shot. ♪♫

Although the Beatles disbanded in 1970, their music continues to capture the imagination of their legions of fans, attract new listeners, and influence popular music and musicians worldwide.

occasion John and Paul wrote "All You Need Is Love," which became a virtual anthem for the flower-power, antiwar generation of the 1960s. It had universal appeal to both young and old and, not surprisingly, became a number-one hit.

Songs of protest and of social consciousness had begun to take hold in the early 1960s, following in the earlier tradition of such notables as Woody Guthrie and Pete Seeger. Youth was beginning to rise up against problems they saw not being taken seriously by mainstream society: the nuclear threat, needless war, civil-rights abuse, and environmental desecration, among others. Seeger, along with Phil Ochs and Tom Paxton, were among the early folk voices expressing this dissent. By the mid-1960s, the civil rights and the anti–Vietnam War movements fueled a youth movement supporting peace, freedom, nonviolence, and love of fellow man. These ideas were put to song by Joan Baez, Simon and Garfunkel, Bob Dylan, and many others.

Dylan in particular gathered a huge counterculture following that formed part of the core of youth protests of the 1960s. Dylan's song "Blowin' in the Wind" became a classic, echoing the mood of the sixties with its railing against racism and war.

A substantial and highly visible part of the 1960s' youth movement were the hippies, who banded together in an alternative lifestyle that demonstrated their disagreement with conventional society and the way it dealt with the social ills of the period. Often shunning work, hippies tended to wander freely, lived with few restrictions, and dressed in a nonconformist fashion that often featured secondhand clothing. Drugs, notably marijuana and LSD, were characteristically used and advocated by the hippies. They typically staged or joined into protests against the Vietnam War and demonstrations for civil rights and other causes.

The flower children, an outgrowth of the hippie movement, particularly advocated nonviolence, peace, and love. They lived close to nature and often wore flowers in their hair and sometimes they handed out flowers in the street.

Although centered in the United States, the youth movement had manifestations in Britain and other countries. Musical groups of the 1960s, including many rock groups, joined into this scene, giving expression to the themes of the hippies, the flower children, and the youth movement in general. Not the least of these groups from the mid-1960s on were the Beatles.

It was within this atmosphere of change and questioning of social values that George and his wife, Pattie, began immersing themselves in Eastern philosophy and mysticism, and they had made contact with several gurus, or spiritual teachers. Their enthusiasm peaked when they encountered the teachings of the Maharishi Mahesh Yogi, who headed a philosophical movement called transcendental meditation. When the Maharishi appeared in London for a lecture, George and Pattie not only attended but persuaded the other Beatles to come along as well. They all came away excited and, at the Maharishi's invitation, determined that they would join him for a ten-day orientation in Bangor, Wales.

The Beatles traveled with the Maharishi on the train trip to Bangor, during which they were exposed to the wisdom of the guru. Word had gotten out that the Beatles were coming to Bangor, and when they arrived there was an outbreak of Beatlemania, to which they were growing unaccustomed. A few days later the Beatles received news that shocked them as nothing had since Stu Sutcliffe's death: Brian Epstein was dead. It appeared he had taken an overdose of drugs, but the death was deemed accidental. The evidence would seem to confirm this, but there is also reason to believe that Brian's drug use had grown as he saw his control of the Beatles slipping away. More and more he had relied on the use of sedatives and sleeping pills as he sought a new outlet for his creative management skills. His death may not have been deliberate, but in a way, after touring stopped, the willful path he chose led to death.

The Beatles' reliance on Brian had been diminishing after they ended touring and began developing their own projects as a group and individually. Accordingly, although Brian's death caused them much personal grief, it did not affect their professional life as much as it would have a year earlier. There was a limit, too, as to how close the Beatles could be with Brian because he was a homosexual and his social life was mostly apart from theirs. Nevertheless, the boys had wanted Brian to join them in Bangor for their transcendental meditation course, and he had agreed, before his death intervened.

After Brian's passing, the boys' enthusiasm for the Maharishi and transcendental meditation went unabated. The holy man invited them to join him for a three-month retreat in India, which they agreed to do beginning the following February. In the meantime, they were eager to start work on a project that stemmed largely from Paul. It was a movie that they would produce themselves through a new company they had formed called Apple Corps, Ltd., which was to have many branches, including filmmaking and recording.

The film, designed for television, would be called *Magical Mystery Tour*, and it would be largely improvised. The film was conceived as a bus trip through England that takes on fantastical and surreal proportions. On the bus are the cast and crew, including the Beatles and many of their friends and associates, all of whom take part in the film. Six new Beatles songs were written for the venture.[1]

Magical Mystery Tour was presented on British television in December 1967. It bombed, and the critics had a field day panning it. But in the end it was not a bad effort for a bunch of guys who had never produced a movie before. It was received a little better in the United States and other places, and some latter-day reviewers have rated it more highly. Paul and some others later felt it may have been ahead of its time.

The sound-track album was also regarded largely as a

relative downturn in the Beatles' musical quality. Nevertheless it produced some good music, including John's "I Am the Walrus," which became a best-seller as a single with Paul's hit "Hello Goodbye" on the A side. The Beatles were still somewhat in their psychedelic phase at the time of the recording; it was a period during which George Martin referred to some of their work as "disorganized chaos."[2] Despite its lack of uniform quality, however, the album was a hot seller that resulted in another number-one Beatles hit.

During early 1968, the Beatles were involved in various musical projects individually and as a group. George Harrison, in particular, broke away for an independent venture in which he wrote and produced the musical score for a film called *Wonderwall*. The music bore the stamp of George's Indian influence, and much of it was, in fact, recorded in Bombay, India. A sound-track album, *Wonderwall Music*, was also recorded and produced by George. No matter their various involvements, in mid-February all the Beatles broke away for an extended retreat in India, in response to the Maharishi's invitation. They were all looking forward to a stay of a couple of months, but it was not to be so.

After only about ten days, Ringo and Maureen had had it with the spicy food and the routine, and they returned to England. Paul and Jane Asher hung on for about five weeks before checking out. The Harrisons and the Lennons, however, remained for almost ten weeks before they became disillusioned with the Maharishi. They had thought him a godlike person, above the normal human temptations. They found, however, that he was quite human, interested in materialistic things, and even, as they construed it, a fancier of the opposite sex.

Although the Beatles gave up on the Maharishi, they felt they had derived substantial benefits from transcendental meditation. Most significantly, during this period they gave up drugs in deference to meditation. Through their experience they found a new creative energy within themselves that blossomed into one of their most fruitful periods of musical production. It also helped them recover from the loss of Brian. John, waxing philosophical after their manager's death, said, "Well, Brian is just passing into the next phase. . . . His spirit is still around and always will be."[3]

Much of the material for their next album was written while in their meditative mode during the first half of 1968. Their musical efforts during that period resulted in what is known popularly as the White Album, although properly titled *The Beatles*. It was their first double-disc album, and it was packaged in an almost solidly white record jacket. Recording began in late May 1968 and took five months to complete.

Although they produced some of their finest work for the album, it was a long and difficult project that saw the Beatles frequently at odds with one another. Ringo even walked out for one two-week period. Part of the problem was that the boys were feeling increasingly independent from the group. Also, Paul had tried to become their artistic director, as well as taking over some of Brian's role, and was at times insufferably overbearing. There was yet another fly in the ointment. Her name was Yoko Ono. Yoko affected John in a most profound way almost from the outset. He once said, "As she was talking to me I would get high, and the discussion would get to such a level that I would be goin' higher and higher. When she'd leave I'd go back to this sort of suburbia."[4]

Yoko Ono was an American-educated Japanese avant-garde artist whose work was on exhibit at a London gallery when she met John in November 1966. After the meeting at the gallery, Yoko pursued John relentlessly, and John became more and more fascinated with her intelligence, artistic wisdom, and wit. In the spring of 1968, they began having an affair, and soon afterward John and Cyn separated. From that time on, John and Yoko were bonded to one another with a dynamic human chemistry that virtually shut everything else out.

Yoko became sort of a fifth Beatle, not that anyone but John was really eager to have her involved in the group's affairs. John, however, insisted on having Yoko at his side at all times on both a personal and a professional level. He was reported to have stated, "Yoko is now part of me. In other words, as I have a right and a left hand, so I have Yoko, and wherever I am, she is."[5] Yoko was highly regarded for her imaginative art skills and still pursued her own career, but now she was an integral part of John's career as well.

Having Yoko always around both in the studio and at Apple Corps eventually started to grate on the other Beatles and the corporate employees. There is little doubt that her presence widened the rift that was beginning to develop in the Beatles. Mark Lewisohn is quoted as saying that the Yoko-John union "had an undeniably negative bearing on the functioning of the Beatles as a unit."[6] More importantly, through Yoko John was finding a new voice and a new self; she was giving direction to his life, and a purpose and fulfillment that was becoming more difficult for him to find as a Beatle.

The White Album came out in November 1968, and Yoko's influence did not, hinder its commercial value. The album shot right to number one on both U.S. and British charts. Most of the material on the two-record, thirty-track album was written while the Beatles were on their retreat in India. It included some memorable Beatles hits, including "Back in the U.S.S.R.," "Glass Onion," "Julia" (dedicated to John's mother), "Sexy Sadie" (John's parody of the Maharishi), "Helter Skelter," and the George Harrison classic, "While My Guitar Gently Weeps" (featuring Eric Clapton's splendid lead guitar).

Prior to the White Album, the Beatles had been involved in the production of a full-length animated feature film called *Yellow Submarine*. The Beatles are portrayed in the film as principal characters who, with Old Fred and his yellow submarine, help rid Pepperland of the evil Blue Meanies. The Beatles provided some of the sound-track music for the venture, which included four new songs and some of their earlier work. The title song had been issued as a single in 1966, and there were a number of pieces from *Sgt. Pepper*. The sound-track album from the movie was produced by the Beatles and released in January 1969, and although successful, it was not a number-one hit. George Martin was the musical director for the film.

While John was being obsessed, if not possessed, by Yoko, Paul was trying to continue the Beatles tradition. If John had become the avant-garde, Paul, while growing artistically, remained the old guard, attempting to stay with their successful formula and expand on it through Apple Corps and other ventures. It was Paul who, sensing that they might split up, tried to persuade the group to perform live again as a way of regaining their spirit and unity. The others, particularly John and George, wouldn't hear of it. Paul took over artistic leadership of the group because John's outside interests with Yoko were now primary with him, and George and Ringo were distracted by their own activities.

Paul also continued his songwriting in the old tradition, while John was now trying to send socially significant messages to the world. Not to say the two no longer worked together. The songwriting bond between them still remained strong, even as they quarreled over other things. No better example of the breach in their writing style, however, is more clear than on the single released in August 1968, "Hey Jude" / "Revolution." The A side was Paul's "Hey Jude," a sentimental piece that spoke of finding happiness, a kind of looking for the bluebird, but with more substance. John's "Revolution," on the other hand, was a cry for peaceful change, for a better society without war. But he was ambivalent in the song about his own involvement if a just cause required violence.

John had been getting more and more interested in the causes of the late 1960s, including peace, religion, social apathy, and the need for more love between peoples of the world. This concern with issues, especially the peace issue, became more intense after his liaison with Yoko. John and Yoko, in fact, drew great attention to the peace movement with their Bed-Ins For Peace in Amsterdam and, later, in Toronto. In each case, they remained in bed for several days during which they allowed themselves to be photographed and interviewed. Songs John wrote or was involved in writing that expressed his concern and social consciousness in various areas included "Revolution," "Nowhere Man," "A Day In The Life," "All You Need Is Love," "Give Peace a Chance," "Working Class Hero," "God," and "Love."

Both "Revolution" and "Hey Jude" were outstanding, and George Martin observed that the disc really had two A sides. The recording became one of the best-selling singles of all time and the all-time best-selling Beatles single. But it was "Hey Jude" that took the charts by storm, hitting number one in Britain and the United States and remaining number one on the U.S. *Billboard* charts a record nine weeks. Moreover, although it was John who was preaching the message of the sixties youth revolt, it was "Hey Jude" that was adopted as a kind of theme song of camaraderie for the period's youth movement.

The seven-minute playing time of "Hey Jude" was a record for the time and was distinguished by its progressive build through the layering of instruments and voices. By its finale, a full orchestra had been brought in along with the 300 voices of a "studio" audience that had been invited to participate. A promotional video of the recording showing the crowd all pressed together with the Beatles and swaying to the final resounding chorus was at least part of the reason it hit home with sixties youth. (The promotional videos the Beatles made are considered the forerunners of the videos seen today on MTV.)

The interpersonal relationships of the Beatles were rocky in 1968, and things continued to slide in 1969 and 1970. During 1968 the boys had to face their first business failure as their Apple Corps venture, except for the record division, had to be closed down. That caused considerable dissension, but there were other disruptions as well. John, who had shown artistic promise in school, was now attracted to the art world, and encouraged by Yoko, he began exhibiting his own art. The couple also made films and records, including their *Two Virgins* album, which had a highly controversial jacket showing John and Yoko in the nude. George, in the meantime, was spatting with Paul because he felt his compositions were not being featured enough, and when Paul criticized his guitar playing, George walked out briefly. Ringo, fed up with the infighting, announced he was quitting the group but returned after a cooling down.

Paul also had found a new love interest, Linda Eastman. Paul was at a press conference in New York promoting Apple Corps when he met Linda, a photographer and the daughter of an affluent copyright lawyer. At the time, Paul was engaged to Jane Asher, but he was irresistibly drawn to Linda, and by July 1968 the engagement with Jane was off. In November, Paul beckoned Linda to London to live with him. Theirs was a more conventional relationship than John and Yoko's, but no less binding. By March of the next year they were married.

Linda did not move into Paul's professional life to the degree that Yoko did John's, but she was also strong and decisive. Implications are that she and Yoko clashed, adding another complicating factor to the Beatles' rapidly deteriorating unity.

The Beatles produced two more major albums as a unit: *Abbey Road*, released in September 1969, and *Let It Be*, released in April 1970. Although it had a later release date, *Let It Be* was actually recorded earlier. It was to be a film/album combination, the film being a documentary on the making of an album. The most memorable moment in the project came in January 1969 when the Beatles played their now-famous rooftop concert atop the Twickenham Studios in London, where the film was being produced. For one of the scenes, the Beatles were filmed playing on the studio's roof. On that chilly January day, loudspeakers blared Beatles music to the astonished lunchtime crowd below, who could not see them. It was the last time the Beatles played before a "live" audience.

Abbey Road, as the name indicates, was recorded at the old EMI studio where they started and which now houses the Beatles archive containing hundreds of hours of their recordings, much of which has never been released. The album was their swan song. Mark Hertsgaard calls the music of the album "as inspired and masterful as any in their career." Indeed, the album proved that their musical evolution and maturity was continuing. *Abbey Road* was another smash hit, dominating the number-one spot on the *Billboard* chart for eleven weeks. The unique synergy of the Fab Four was still there, and probably always would be—as long as they hung together. Unfortunately for the musical world, that was not to be.

There are as many theories as to why the Beatles broke up as there are people who propound them. Nobody, not even the Beatles, really, truly knows why. There was Yoko, there was Linda, there were the separate projects and interests pulling them in different directions, and there was the sniping and quarreling over their business arrangements. John and Paul had interests in a music publishing company called Northern Songs over which they had a dispute. Paul, it appears, had been buying up extra shares of the company unbeknownst to John, who saw this as a betrayal. John was furious over the incident, and it expanded the growing gap between them. With John's new interests developing rapidly, he announced to Apple management in late 1969 that he planned to leave the group but was persuaded not to announce it at that time because of sensitive contract negotiations that were going on.

The final schism, however, came over the issue of who would manage Apple, the Beatles' recording company. John, George, and Ringo wanted Allen Klein, a business-man who had extensive dealings, some of them question-able, in the music world. Paul wanted his father-in-law, attorney Lee Eastman, to be involved. Klein and Eastman worked together for a time, but the tension between them was unremittingly intense. By the end of 1969, it was all coming apart at the seams. Feeding the flames of dissent was another dispute that arose when Paul wanted his own album, *McCartney*, released before *Let It Be*. Ultimately Paul won out, and his album came out in April 1970, just a few weeks before the last Beatles album was released.

Paul tried to turn the others against Klein, who he felt was defrauding them, but to no avail. Paul asked his fellow Beatles to release him from the Beatles partnership. They did not respond. Finally, in an effort to separate himself from Klein, Paul sued in December 1970 to dissolve the partnership. Unfortunately, the other three Beatles had to be named in the suit, not Klein. In January 1971, the court ruled in favor of Paul, and the Beatles' partnership was ended.[7] A final irony: several years later all four ex-Beatles sued Klein for fraud.

It was a sad day for music. A very sad day, indeed. The four young men who had revolutionized pop music would never play as a group again. Their musical influence, how-ever, did not end, and it still goes on to this day.

NINETEEN

LiFE iN THE AFTERGLOW

When they were together they seemed to become another dimension.
—George Martin, quoted by Mark Hertsgaard in the
New Yorker, January 24, 1994

From 1970, the Beatles were off in separate, but not always unrelated, directions. For all of them music remained a dominating force in their lives, and after some of the bitterness of their business split cooled down, their paths inevitably crossed, and their relations were amicable for the most part. One thing for sure: the world would never let them forget that they were once the Beatles. Although they were all variably successful in their post-Beatles lives, none could match their accomplishments as the Beatles. In 1988, the Beatles were admitted into the Rock 'n' Roll Hall of Fame.

JOHN

When the Beatles split in 1970, John was already off in a new direction. He would never write another song with Paul. His new partner was Yoko Ono. The two were married in March 1969, soon after Yoko was divorced from her first husband. To symbolize his devotion to Yoko, John changed his middle name from Winston to Ono. The major thrust of John's creative life from then on was toward the production of avant-garde or socially conscious art, film, and music.

The couple made a number of recordings and live appearances under the name Plastic Ono Band. It was not a permanent group but often included Eric Clapton on lead guitar and Klaus Voormann on bass. John also brought in George and Ringo for some recordings, but not necessarily together. John became one of the 1960s peace movement's best-known spokespersons, and his music often reflected his inner feelings. The first recording by the Plastic Ono Band was "Give Peace a Chance." Other titles were "Cold Turkey," "Instant Karma," and "Power to the People." Their albums included *John Lennon\Plastic Ono Band*, *Imagine*, *Some Time in New York City*, and *Mind Games*. John and Yoko's work achieved varying artistic and commercial success.

John and Yoko spent most of their time in the United States, making New York City their home. After attending to the legal dissolution of the Beatles in 1971, John never returned to his homeland. In the early 1970s, John and Yoko also spent considerable time attempting to gain custody of Yoko's daughter, Kyoko, from her first husband. Yoko was eventually awarded custody, but Kyoko still stayed mostly with her father. Their quest for Kyoko may have been psychologically motivated by Yoko's several miscarriages with John.

John and Yoko sought to extend their U.S. visa privileges, but U.S. immigration authorities began deportation proceedings on drug-related grounds. John fought the deportation, claiming that it was politically based. During this period, in the early 1970s, the Vietnam War was raging. John was an outspoken critic of the war, and he earned the displeasure of President Richard M. Nixon's administration, which feared that he was influencing American youth. John claimed that his phone lines were illegally tapped and that the Nixon administration had a vendetta against him. (His suspicions were borne out by documents made public in 1995.) With his attorney, John fought the government's deportation attempt, and with a groundswell of support from the media and a strong legal defense, John won the case in October 1975. He then became a permanent resident of the United States.

Prior to the immigration victory, John had gone through what may have been the most agonizing period of his life. In the fall of 1974 John and Yoko separated. It was Yoko's idea. John had fallen into a syndrome of self-pity abetted by drug and alcohol abuse. It was a cycle into which John was becoming more and more deeply ensconced, and Yoko knew John had to get away in order to find himself.

John could not disagree. He would say later, "I was behaving stupidly, pure and simple. . . . It was grow-up time and I'm glad she made me do it." There was also the problem of two sensitive artists living together, spending almost every minute together. "It was bound to happen we'd snap," said John.[1]

John headed for Los Angeles. In his company was a highly competent and loyal secretary who had worked for John and Yoko in their New York apartment; her name was May Pang. There has been some controversy over the nature of the relationship between John and May Pang. In Ray Coleman's biography of John, it is contended that Yoko encouraged May to go with John. She knew that John was relatively helpless in handling his day-to-day affairs and that a romantic relationship might develop, but she felt John needed May to get along.[2]

May agrees that Yoko encouraged her to go with John. "I didn't like the idea of going with John," May said in a 1995 interview. Recalling their discussion, May said that Yoko told her "I don't want to see John go off with someone who won't be very nice to him," most likely referring to the female companionship he might encounter in the la-la-land of Hollywood. May agreed to the arrangement.[3]

John and May lived together for a year and a half, in

New York and in Los Angeles. John would call this break-up period his "lost weekend." Finding himself suddenly free of marital restrictions, he pursued a wild, unrestricted, and besotted lifestyle in Los Angeles. Through it, seemingly, he rid his body of a lot of pent-up emotional poison and did some growing up that he missed at an earlier age.

Remarkably, John made an album during this period, which was not outstanding but at least produced an excellent single, "Whatever Gets You Thru the Night." The recording was made with Elton John, who predicted it would reach number one. John scoffed, but the record did become John's first solo number one. To repay Elton, John performed with him in concert at Madison Square Garden on Thanksgiving night, 1974. That concert appearance seemingly was a springboard for John to get his life back on track.

In early 1975, Yoko let John back in the house. He had had a romantic interlude with May Pang, as revealed in her book, *Loving John*, but his love for Yoko endured, and it was just a matter of time until they were reunited. Yoko became pregnant shortly after his return, and John, in a burst of creative energy, produced a new album, *Rock 'n' Roll*. In it he revisited many of the songs from the early days in Liverpool and Hamburg. Yoko gave birth to a boy, Sean, on October 9, John's birthday. Afterward, John abruptly dropped out of the music scene.

For the following five years, he became, in his own words, "a house husband," completely devoting himself to wife and child. Then near the end of 1980, John and Yoko suddenly surged back, cutting two more albums, *Double Fantasy* and *Milk and Honey*. John's return caused great excitement. John and Yoko began visiting the studio almost daily to rehearse and record. He was again driven by his unique creative urge, but now he was on an even keel, working steadily to accomplish his goals.

On the night of December 8, 1980, John and Yoko returned from the studio just before 11:00 P.M. As they left their car and walked toward their apartment, a voice called out John's name. Before John could turn, a demented assassin raised a pistol and pumped several bullets into his back. The police arrived to find John slumped to the ground, Yoko at his side. They rushed him to the hospital, but it was too late. John Lennon was dead at the age of 39.

In 1994, John Lennon was elected to the Rock and Roll Hall of Fame. In its coverage of that ceremony, *Rolling Stone* magazine stated: "Quite simply, there is no figure more important in the history of rock & roll than John Lennon. . . . His impact remains universal, his influence undiminished."

PAUL

Even before the breakup, Paul had issued his own solo album, *McCartney*. Paul went on to write more music and produce more records than any of the other ex-Beatles after the breakup. Like John, he incorporated his wife, Linda, into his musical life as a singer and keyboardist. Some reviewers question whether either Yoko or Linda really possess the musical talent to play alongside their husbands. Critics were not usually kind to either. For Paul and Linda it was rocky going at first. Paul's first solo album, *McCartney*, was not well received critically and neither was his second, *Ram*, which also featured Linda.

After those first solo rebuffs, Paul decided to form a band and return to the live concert circuit, which he loved and had implored the Beatles to do before the breakup. The group Paul formed in 1971 to go on tour was dubbed Wings. The personnel for Wings changed over the years, but it usually included Linda. Wings had some trouble flying at first, but by the mid-1970s the group was doing well. Paul's albums from that period include *Wild Life*, *Red Rose Speedway*, *Band on the Run*, and *Venus and Mars*. None made the critics rave, but there were individual high spots, and all achieved some degree of commercial success. *Band on the Run*, in fact, received two Grammy Awards in the United States.

No question Paul had the popular touch and could strike the right notes in the music market. He had demonstrated this with the Beatles, only then John's influence kept the songs from being too cute. Likewise, Paul kept John's work from being overserious. Their great songwriting as a team was seldom equalled by either as a solo artist.

Paul continued to write music and produce records right into the 1990s, never giving an indication that he had any intention of quitting. His incredible artistic drive resulted in an extensive post-Beatles live performance career and discography. He has contemplated an end to touring from time to time, but always the urge would come back and he would find himself on the road. In 1994 he launched a New World Tour playing seventy-eight concerts throughout Europe, the United States, the United Kingdom, Japan, and South America. Near the end of that tour in South America he told *Rolling Stone*, "in the old days, we did maybe half-hour shows. . . . Now I find myself 30 years older, doing more than a two-hour show. . . . It's . . . nuts, but obviously I must love it."[4]

Paul had disbanded Wings in 1983 after they had made eight more albums and many singles. In the meantime, he followed other pursuits, producing records for other talent, including George and Ringo, and establishing his own highly profitable music publishing business. Paul also lent his support to charitable projects.

From the time Linda began living with Paul in 1968 they were hardly ever apart, and the McCartney clan grew considerably. Paul had become an instant "father" when they married, Linda having a seven-year-old daughter, Heather, from a previous marriage. The McCartneys followed up with three more children, two daughters, Mary (1969), and Stella (1971), and a son, James (1977). Linda and Paul became dedicated vegetarians during their marriage, and they turned their commitment into a family business. Linda wrote a vegetarian cookbook that became a best-seller, and she started a company that produces a line of vegetarian products sold under the Linda McCartney name. The McCartneys retain a residence in London, mainly for business, but their main home is an estate and farm in Scotland.

GEORGE

After the 1970 breakup, George continued to be fascinated with the music and philosophy of the East, his disappointing experience with the Maharishi notwithstanding. The Indian influence would continue to mark his musical life. His interest in the Hare Krishna movement resulted in a Harrison-produced LP, *The Hare Krishna Mantra* in 1969.

George had been very frustrated during the last years of the Beatles partnership. His own songwriting had become quite prolific, but it found little outlet on Beatles records. By 1970, he had a huge backlog, and it finally burst forth in a triple album, *All Things Must Pass*. "Especially after 1966," he told *Rolling Stone* in an interview, "I was starting to write loads of tunes, and one or two songs per album (with the Beatles) wasn't sufficient for me."[5] *All Things* was George's third solo album, after *Wonderwall* and a 1969 effort, *Electronic Sounds*, a studio experiment in new sounds that didn't go anywhere. *All Things* received wide critical acclaim, and one of its tracks, "My Sweet Lord," hit number one on the *Billboard* chart, remaining there for four weeks.

George's next major project was one that came from the heart. Ravi Shankar came to George in 1971 with an idea for raising money to aid Bangladesh, a country then suffering massively from the effects of a civil war. George, characteristically compassionate and harboring a special interest in the Indian subcontinent, took the project far beyond Ravi's dreams. It became the Concert for Bangladesh, which was held in New York City's Madison Square Garden in August 1971. The concert included some of the biggest names in rock and pop: George Harrison, Ravi Shankar, Eric Clapton, Ringo Starr, and Bob Dylan. A tape and an album were made from the concert, parlaying the affair into a $15 million donation to the war-torn country.[6]

The benefit concert was one of George's rare concert appearances after the Beatles broke up. Like John, but unlike Paul and Ringo, he had had enough of live appearances with the Beatles and was content to work in the studio and find new interests. He established his own record label, Dark Horse, in the mid-1970s, which produced many of his own and other artist's records. George also became interested in film production and in 1978 co-founded a film company called HandMade. The company has had its ups and downs, but some really fine and commercially successful films were produced, including *The Life of Brian*, *Time Bandits*, *Mona Lisa*, and *Monty Python and the Holy Grail*. The company also has had some clunkers, most notably *Shanghai Surprise*, featuring Madonna and her then-husband, Sean Penn. The film was soundly ripped by the critics.[7]

After *All Things Must Pass*, George's records received relatively spotty acclaim. He, like the other ex-Beatles, could not turn out hits one after another as the Beatles had. It wasn't until November 1987, with the release of his album *Cloud Nine*, that George reached a degree of acclaim comparable to that of *All Things*. For *Cloud Nine* he gathered an all-star group of musicians, including Elton John and Eric Clapton, who is often cited as his best friend. The album brought George back into the limelight as one of rock's top talents.

George's personal life also had its rocky moments as well. The death of his mother in 1970 and his father in 1978 were difficult times. His married life with Pattie also ran into rough waters. Despite their shared interest in Eastern philosophy, the marriage started coming apart in the early 1970s. They had no children, and Pattie may have been bored living in the isolation of their Friar Park, Oxfordshire, mansion.

A romance began between Pattie and Eric Clapton, and

eventually she left George for his close pal. In 1977, Pattie divorced George and two years later married Eric. Nevertheless, the couple and George managed to remain good friends—possibly a reflection of his philosophical studies. In fact, George played at the newlyweds' wedding reception.

In the meantime, George met Olivia Arias, who had been born in Mexico and educated in the United States. She worked as George's secretary in Los Angeles at Dark Horse records in 1974, and soon they became romantically involved. In August 1978, they had a son, Dhani, and were married the following month, an earlier wedding having been postponed by Harold Harrison's death.

RiNGo

After the breakup, Ringo told *People* magazine in 1976, "I sat in my garden for about a year wondering what on earth was going to happen to me. I was sick." Ringo probably took the breakup harder than the others because he had the least idea of the direction he wanted his life to take.[8] He couldn't just join another band, because he was so much more famous than any band he could join. He was interested in movies and had already had some successful roles prior to the breakup. Propelled by his acclaimed work in *A Hard Day's Night* and *Help!*, Ringo had substantial roles in *Candy* (1968), *The Magic Christian* (1969), and *Blindman* (1971).

Creatively Ringo had been mostly in the background as a Beatle. But after the breakup, he emerged to make several commercially successful solo recordings in the early 1970s. In 1970 he received moderate acclaim for *Sentimental Journey*, a nostalgic collection of standards produced by George Martin. Ringo then did something strange for an Englishman, he made a country-and-western album. He had always loved country and western, so when an opportunity came he went to Nashville and cut *Beaucoups of Blues*.

A year later he composed "It Don't Come Easy," which became a hit single produced by, and featuring the guitar of, George Harrison. It was in 1973, however, that Ringo made his first hit album, *Ringo*, also featuring George and the other ex-Beatles, but not as a foursome. It went to number two on the *Billboard* chart.[9]

In the following years, however, Ringo's moments of triumph were infrequent. A few records made it into the top ten, but there seemed to be no consistent progression. He managed to be cast in a few films, but they were low-budget flicks that drew little attention. An exception was *Caveman* (1979), which was still not a critical triumph but had fair commercial success. Perhaps more significantly, his costar on the film was Barbara Bach, who became the second Mrs. Starkey.[10] During this period, he was also making occasional guest appearances on television and even had his own TV special, "Ringo." One activity for which he received praise but not much fame was his voice-over for a children's series, *Thomas the Tank Engine*, which has been acclaimed in the children's field.

Ringo's experience with his own children may have helped him in his video work. He and Maureen parented three children: Zak (1965), Jason (1967), and their only daughter, Lee (1970). The marriage seemed very solid until the early 1970s when rumors of a George/Maureen affair, complicated by Ringo's excessive living, tore the couple apart. They were divorced in 1975, and in 1981 Ringo married his second wife, Barbara Bach.

With his career problems, Ringo had relied increasingly on drugs and alcohol for support, which only intensified his problems. His 1981 album, *Stop and Smell the Roses*, released after John's death, was moderately received. It represented a kind of farewell to the past and was, perhaps, a springboard to better things for Ringo.

Barbara and Ringo both entered a drug-alcohol rehabilitation program in the late 1980s, and after a respite in activities, Ringo bounced back into music with renewed vigor. In 1989 he assembled the All-Starr Band, taking it on an extensive tour to the United States and Japan. The tour was highly successful and prompted Ringo to reform the band for additional tours in the 1990s. Among the featured All-Starrs in the band was Ringo's own son Zak on drums. Ringo has continued his recording career, receiving some critical praise for his *Time Takes Time* album in 1992, and he has also had some success doing television commercials. Three decades along a bumpy road from the Beatles' breakup, Ringo's career is looking up.

EPILOGUE
BEATLEMANIA REVISITED

Whatever happened to the life that we once knew?
Always made me feel free as a bird.
        —from "Free as a Bird" (Lennon-McCartney),
                                The Beatles Anthology, 1995

We were just a band that made it very, very big, that's all.
                —John Lennon, *The Beatles Anthology 1*, 1995

For a quarter century the speculation went on. Would the Beatles ever get back together? When? Where? How? Would they ever appear live? Could they be great without John? Was the old magic still there? To the latter question, the year 1995 answered "yes," with a bang. Other speculation also ended as new and never before released Beatles material hit the market with overwhelming success. The dream year for Beatles fans was 1995: it was the year that bore the fruit of the Beatles' reunion in the studio. The new music they recorded was introduced on a television series and a new double album, both marketed in November 1995.

In the decades following the breakup, EMI and Capitol periodically repackaged previously released Beatles material and promoted it to a public eager to grasp at any straw of a Beatles revival. Promotional campaigns also accompanied each major Beatles anniversary. There always has been and continues to be enough latent Beatlemania out there for each promotion to set off a buying frenzy that would rocket Beatles recordings back onto the charts. Sales would subside, but most Beatles tapes and CDs have continued to be available at record stores on a regular basis, indicating a consistent level of popularity. In fact, *Rolling Stone* reported that "Beatles recordings still accounted for nearly 40 percent of the label's [Capitol's] sales well into the 1990s." The band's appeal, it was also reported, extended to all age groups.[1]

The latest resurgence of Beatlemania began with the release of the group's first album of previously unreleased material since 1970. *Live at the BBC* hit the market in late 1994 and had a brief fling at the top of the charts despite the relatively primitive nature of some of its content. The double album consists of fifty-five selections from the Beatles' fifty-two BBC radio performances, spanning 1962 to 1965. It reflects at times an early, less mature state of the group's musical growth in which they belted out American rock numbers more frequently than their own compositions, which were to become the hallmark of their greater success and their enduring legacy. Old and new Beatles fans made the album an unqualified success, buying up some eight million copies worldwide in the first year of its release.[2]

Overcoming the sound quality produced on the BBC's unsophisticated equipment had been a problem, and the reproduction hardly compares with their high-tech studio recordings. But if the album does not exhibit the polish of the studio, it still holds a rich sampling of a talented group having fun with the music that gave Beatlemania its early impetus. The tracks are spiced with typically dry-witted Beatles banter, providing a good measure of their trademark humor.

It was also in 1994 that the three remaining Beatles returned to the studio and recorded music together for the first time in twenty-five years. Even John was present via tapes, donated by Yoko, that he had made in the late 1970s. Paul and George added some lyrics to John's incomplete "Free as a Bird," and the four came together again electronically, cutting a new record for the first time in almost twenty-five years. A second such effort was made with another Lennon cut, "Real Love." The song had appeared in the John-Yoko film *Imagine*, but reportedly a different track was provided by Yoko.

The two new singles became part of a monster-sized Beatles multimedia project that exploded onto a Beatles-craving public in November 1995, following a massive publicity campaign. Called *The Beatles Anthology*, its grand plan projected a six-hour television special, double-disc albums, home videos, books, and rerelease of the group's previous albums. The whole package could generate as much as $250 million in revenue according to a *Rolling Stone* magazine source.

The Beatles blitz of 1995 began with the television documentary, the official television biography of the Beatles that they sanctioned and produced themselves, telling their story as they wish it to be told. It includes rare old footage along with new commentary by the three living Beatles and many of their associates from earlier years, including George Martin, the late Brian Epstein, and Neil Aspinall, a school chum of the Beatles who now heads Apple Corps Ltd. Aspinall was a driving force behind the anthology project, as he has been with other Beatles releases and business.

The documentary, a three-part, six-hour series, was an unqualified success. Television companies worldwide leaped into the bidding for rights to broadcast the biography, which was booked into more than forty countries. In the United States, ABC paid almost $20 million for rights to show the product to the American public, and sponsors paid more than $300,000 for some thirty-second commercials. It was reportedly the fastest-selling special in the network's history.[3] Throughout the world, it was bought sight unseen, purely on the basis of the Beatles' reputation.

The album was released in tandem with the TV special. Called *The Beatles Anthology 1* (two more anthologies were scheduled to follow in 1996), it begins with "Free as a Bird" and commentary by John Lennon. After that the record traces the Beatles' development from their very earliest extant recorded beginnings. It includes a 1958 cut of Buddy Holly's "That'll Be the Day" made by the Quarry Men in a rented Liverpool studio, and their first commercial recording on which they backed Tony Sheridan singing "My Bonnie" in Hamburg in 1961.

Many songs recorded in the next several years follow, concluding with their October 1964 version of "Kansas City" and "Hey - Hey - Hey - Hey." Commentary by the boys and Brian Epstein is interspersed between the cuts, providing additional insights on their musical career. In all, the album has sixty tracks, including some highly amusing recording outtakes. The album's material is largely culled from the Abbey Road archives, a treasure trove of hundreds of hours of unreleased Beatles music. Producing and directing the work was—who else?—George Martin.

One would suppose that at some point the Beatles would quit being phenomenal, perhaps just out of courtesy to the rest of the musical competition. Maybe they will, but the end does not yet seem to be in sight. The foursome has not performed live since 1966, not cut an album since 1970, but they continue to endure as one of the top moneymaking acts in show business.

The new album rocketed out of the starting blocks and whizzed right to the top of the *Billboard* and *Cash Box* charts. It was just like the old days of Beatlemania: fans lined up outside of record stores waiting for them to open on the first day of sale; stores selling out in the first couple of days; the wait for back orders to come in. *Billboard* reported that *Anthology 1* sales hit almost 3 million for November and December alone. The first-day sale of 450,000 was reported to be the largest ever opening-day sale for an album. EMI Capitol Music Group of North America reported that "the Beatles album recorded the biggest first week revenue numbers ever."[4]

It was merely the latest in a long succession of runaway hits that spans the decades. *Forbes* magazine in November 1995 reported that the Beatles were the third highest moneymakers in entertainment in 1994–95. "For sheer money-making durability," the magazine stated, "no one comes close to the Beatles."[5] Possibly the monetary climax to their whole career came in March 1996, when in the wake of the *Anthology* documentary and album release, a consortium of promoters offered them an astounding $225 million for a world tour. They turned it down, refusing to be a watered-down, Johnless Beatles. "The size of the offer is scandalous," said Paul. "But for me the three of us isn't as exciting as the four of us."[6]

That the Beatles are among the top moneymaking artists in performance history is easy to calculate in dollars and cents; why they remain among the top earners decade after decade is difficult and complex. Pop music and artists are not supposed to endure like their classical counterparts. Mostly the big stars flash onto the scene, glow brightly for a year or two, and then fade. A few groups, like the Rolling Stones, have been able to maintain their prowess by hanging together, continuing to perform, and to some degree, evolving in artistry with the times. But no one in pop history has come close to doing what the Beatles have done: continuing to produce hits regularly decades after they quit performing and recording.

Why? Looking into the literature of social historians and musicologists and Beatles specialists, of which there are myriad, the curious student of pop can find all kinds of answers: The huge Beatles fandom, surviving since the 1960s, has a fanatical devotion to their heros and provide an instant market for their products; publicity campaigns by the record companies to promote strategically timed releases, such as the anthologies, incite periodic resurgences of Beatlemania and subsequent record-buying sprees; as the embodiment of the 1960s youth movement, the Beatles continue to be the eternal voice of youth rebellion and social change; the Beatles' wit, charm, cuteness, and charisma span the ages and are revisited annually at Beatles conventions, which keep their images alive.

All of these elements contribute to the group's staying power. But none of it would matter without their incredible group synergetic dynamism as musicians. The music produced by the Beatles is, after all, the very foundation of the Beatles phenomenon. Whole industries have been built around their lasting popularity. Annual conventions draw thousands of fans who come in an almost worshipful way to listen to disciple-like speakers, buy Beatles memorabilia as though they were religious objects, and revel in a kind of neo-Beatlemania.

It is not just the aging baby boomers of the 1960s who make up the Fab Four's following in the 1990s. The Beatles scene receives a constant influx of young people, many of whom were not even born when the Beatles were playing live. Such is the incredible gravitational pull of Beatlemania, at the core of which is the music. But like many of the fans who went to live Beatles concerts, today's fans can lose the music in the hoopla. The group's persisting charisma and clever marketing may have something to do with their extended popularity, but there would be nothing without the body of superb, original music they produced together.

The music of the Beatles is their legacy. That it is vastly popular decades after it was produced is testimony to its enduring quality. It is difficult to put into words why a body of music is great, why it endures. It started as big-beat rock 'n' roll and the balladic yearnings of adolescent love, with simple instrumentation, and evolved into much more. Their music grew beyond the youthful, screeching echos of Beatlemania, developing a maturity and universality that appealed to a wider span of age groups and tastes. Their studio production, especially as represented in such works as *Revolver* and *Sgt. Pepper's Lonely Hearts Club Band*, reflected many themes of the human condition: the foibles of man, the disaster of war, the power of love, loneliness, futility, and hope.

And as their musical ideas grew more complex so did their accompanying instrumentation; by the end of their recording days, all the instruments of the symphony orchestra had become part of their musical expression. Their influence on other musical groups was profound and lasting. With each new Beatles record they sent other competing rock groups scurrying off in new directions. So far did the Beatles come from the simple pop styles of the late 1950s and early 1960s that they instigated what was called a whole new genre of music—art rock.[7] They changed forever the way modern music is composed and played, and they are universally acknowledged to rank among the giants of twentieth-century music.

Indeed, the Beatles came, and music was never the same.

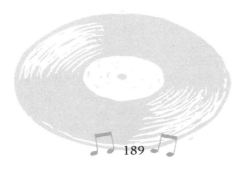

SOURCE NOTES

INTRODUCTION

1. National Public Radio, Weekend Edition, segment no. 18, Saturday, 3 December 1994.

2. Michael Healy, ed., *The Ultimate Encyclopedia of Rock* (New York: HarperPerennial, 1993), pp. 180–81.

3. Peter Gammond, *The Oxford Companion to Popular Music* (New York: Oxford Univ. Press, 1991), p. 46.

4. *Sunday Times* (London), 29 December 1963.

5. *Blade* (Toledo, OH), 3 October 1993, Entertainment and Arts section, p. 1.

6. Charles F. Rosenay, president, Good Day Sunshine: The Beatles Fan Club.

7. America Online, Rec.Music.Beatles.

8. Bonnie Miller, managing editor, *Gold Mine Magazine.*

9. *Chicago Tribune,* 4 December 1994, p. 2; 16 September 1994, p. 2.

10. Tom Schultheiss, ed., *A Day in the Life: The Beatles Day-By-Day 1960–1970* (Ann Arbor, MI: Pierian Press, 1980), p. 109.

11. Ibid., p. 84; *Variety,* 6 January 1965, p. 186.

12. *Variety,* 26 August 1964, p. 43.

13. London *Daily Mirror,* 16 August 1965; *Variety,* 18 August 1965, p.2.

14. *Variety,* 11 October 1967, p. 488.

15. *Melody Maker,* 22 February 1964, p. 10.

16. *Variety,* 13 January 1965, p. 59.

17. *Guinness Book of World Records* (New York: Sterling, 1994), pp. 410–25.

18. *Melody Maker,* 17 December 1994, p. 13; *Billboard,* 24 December 1994.

19. Mark Hertsgaard, "Letting It Be," *New Yorker,* 24 January 1994, p. 87.

PROLOGUE

1. *New York Times,* 8 February 1964, p. 25.

CHAPTER 1

1. Adam Gopnik, "Carry That Weight," *New Yorker,* May 1995, p. 82.

2. David P. Szatmary, *Rockin' in Time: A Social History of Rock and Roll* (New York: Prentice-Hall, 1991), p. 109.

Other sources consulted for this chapter include: Mark Lewisohn, *The Beatles Live* (New York: Henry Holt, 1986); Hunter Davies, *The Beatles: The Authorized Biography* (New York: McGraw Hill, 1968); Philip Norman, *Shout! The Beatles in Their Generation* (New York: Simon and Schuster, 1981); Bill Harry, *The Ultimate Beatles Encyclopedia* (New York: Hyperion, 1992).

CHAPTER 2

1. David Sheff, *Playboy,* January 1981.

2. Ray Coleman, *Lennon: The Definitive Biography* (New York: HarperPerennial, 1992), p. 100.

3. Sheff.

4. Julia Baird with Geoffrey Giuliano, *John Lennon, My Brother* (New York: Henry Holt, 1988), p. 21–22.

5. Coleman, p. 143.

CHAPTER 3

1. Julius Fast, *The Beatles: The Real Story* (New York: Putnam, 1968), p. 38

2. Ibid., p. 39.

3. Hunter Davies, *The Beatles: The Authorized Biography* (New York: McGraw Hill, 1968), p. 27.

4. Ibid., p. 33.

5. "Paul McCartney" in Timothy White, *Rock Lives* (New York: Henry Holt, 1990), pp. 123–24.

CHAPTER 4

1. George Harrison, *I, Me, Mine* (New York: Simon and Schuster, 1980), p. 21.

2. Ibid.

3. Fast, p. 47.

Other sources consulted for this chapter include Hunter Davies, *The Beatles, The Authorized Biography* (New York: McGraw Hill, 1968); Bill Harry, *The Ultimate Beatles Encyclopedia* (New York: Hyperion, 1992); *The Beatles for the Record* (Toronto: Totem Books, 1982); Gareth L. Pawlowski, *How They Became the Beatles* (New York: Dutton, 1989).

CHAPTER 5

1. Jean Shepherd, "The Beatles" (interview), *Playboy*, February 1965.

2. Fast, p. 86.

3. Davies, p. 144.

4. Robyn Flans, "Ringo," *Modern Drumming Magazine*, December 1981/January 1982, p. 10.

5. Ibid.

6. Ibid., p. 12.
7. Ibid., p. 13.
8. Davies, p. 151.

Other sources used in this chapter: *The Beatles for the Record* (Toronto: Totem Books, 1982). Bill Harry, *The Ultimate Beatles Encyclopedia* (New York: Hyperion, 1992).

CHAPTER 6

1. John Lennon, *In His Own Write* (New York: Simon and Schuster, 1964), p. 38.
2. Coleman, p. 129.
3. Harry, p. 67.
4. Lewisohn, pp. 19–26.
5. Baird and Giuliano, pp. 41–42.
6. Davies, p. 56.
7. Lewisohn, p. 20.
8. Baird and Giuliano, p. 44.

CHAPTER 7

1. Harry, p. 489.
2. Davies, p. 64.
3. Schultheiss, p. xvii.
4. Gareth L. Pawlowski, p. 17; Lewisohn, p. 30.
5. Pawlowski, p. 17; Lewisohn, p. 31.
6. Pawlowski, p. 17.

CHAPTER 8

1. Harry, p. 263.
2. Lewisohn, pp. 31–33.
3. Ibid. (from an illustration of a clipping), p. 45.
4. Pawlowski, p. 21.
5. Ibid., p. 25.
6. Mark Hertsgaard, *A Day in the Life: The Music and Artistry of the Beatles* (New York: Delacorte Press, 1995), pp. 42–44.

7. Lewisohn, p. 39.

8. Pawlowski, p. 27.

9. *Mersey Beat,* 20 September/4 October, 1962, p. 40.

CHAPTER 9

1. *Mersey Beat,* 20 June/4 July, 1963, p. 52.

2. Terence John O'Grady, *The Music of the Beatles from 1962 to Sgt. Pepper's Lonely Hearts Club Band,* thesis, University of Wisconsin, Madison, 1975, p. 27.

3. Lewisohn, p. 43.

4. Pawlowski, p. 29.

5. Mersey Beat, p. 52.

6. Cheryl Hill, "The Place Where It All Began," *Datebook,* (Fall 1964), pp. 26–29.

7. Lewisohn, p. 57.

8. Peter McCabe and Robert D. Schonfeld, "4 Boys Who Shook The World," *Sunday Express,* September 17, 1972.

9. Lewisohn, p. 58.

10. Ibid., p. 161.

CHAPTER 10

1. Davies, p. 117.

2. Ibid, p. 124.

3. Lewisohn, p. 66.

4. Ibid.

5. Ibid., p. 68.

6. Brian Epstein, *A Cellarful of Noise* (Garden City, NY: Doubleday, 1964), p. 46.

7. Pete Best and Patrick Doncaster, *Beatle! The Pete Best Story* (New York: Dell, 1985), p. 150.

8. Davies, p. 135.

CHAPTER 11

1. Epstein, p. 53.

2. Davies, p. 162.

3. Lewisohn, pp. 110–14.

4. Best, p. 166.

5. Epstein, p. 58.

6. Davies, p. 46.

7. Ibid. pp. 137–38.

8. Hertsgaard, pp. 30–31.

9. Lewisohn, pp. 103, 118.

CHAPTER 12

1. Valerie Mabbs, "The Beatles Story," *Record Mirror*, 4 June 1972.

2. Ibid.

3. Harry, p. 503.

4. Davies, p. 174.

5. Pawlowski, p. 143.

6. Hertsgaard, p. 51.

7. McCabe and Schonfeld.

8. Davies, pp. 180–81.

CHAPTER 13

1. Davies, p. 181.

2. Ibid., pp. 182–83.

3. Pawlowski, p. 150.

4. Lewisohn, p. 141.

5. Pawlowski, p. 160.

CHAPTER 14

1. Patrick Snyder-Scumpy, "People and Things That Went Before," *Crawdaddy*, June 1973, p. 151.

2. *New York Times*, 17 February 1964, p. 20.

3. Norman, p. 220.

4. Ibid., p. 225.

5. Davies, pp. 196–97.

6. Jack Hutton, *Melody Maker*, 22 February 1964, pp. 10–11.

CHAPTER 15
1. Hertsgaard, p. 75.
2. Pawlowski, p. 188.
3. Davies, p. 203.
4. Ibid.

CHAPTER 16
1. Davies, p. 205.
2. Hertsgaard, pp. 101–3.
3. Harry, p. 444.
4. Herm Schoenfeld, *Variety*, 18 August 1965, p. 2.
5. Lewisohn, p. 184.

CHAPTER 17
1. *Variety*, 6 July 1966, p. 39.
2. Coleman, pp. 405–8.
3. Lewisohn, p. 197.
4. Hertsgaard, p. 203.
5. Fast, p. 222.
6. Hertsgaard, p. 9.
7. Harry, p. 590.
8. Ibid., p. 585.
9. Hertsgaard, pp. 213, 221.

CHAPTER 18
1. Harry, pp. 424–25.
2. Hertsgaard, p. 229; Harry, p. 243.
3. Coleman, p. 431.
4. McCabe and Schonfeld, *The Sunday Express*, 1 October 1972, p. 9.
5. Hertsgaard, p. 239.

6. Ibid., p. 240.

7. Ibid., pp. 287–88.

Chapter 19

1. Coleman, p. 590.

2. Ibid., pp. 591–93.

3. May Pang, interview with author, December 1994.

4. *Rolling Stone,* 10 February 1994, p. 12.

5. *Rolling Stone,* 22 October 1987, p. 42.

6. Geoffery Giuliano, *Dark Horse* (New York: Dutton, 1990), pp. 134–36.

7. Ibid., pp. 182–84

8. *People,* 5 April 1976, p. 18.

9. *Contemporary Musicians* (Detroit: Gale Research, 1994), Volume 10, pp. 236–37.

10. William McKeen, *The Beatles: A Bio-Bibliography* (Westport, CT: Greenwood Press, 1989), p. 84.

Epilogue

1. Jerry McCuller, *Rolling Stone,* 30 November 1995, pp. 26, 28.

2. *The Beatles Monthly Book,* October 1995, p. 34.

3. *Forbes,* 25 September 1995, p. 130.

4. *Chicago Tribune,* 1 December 1995, p. 2.

5. *Forbes,* p. 133.

6. *Chicago Tribune,* 5 March 1996, p. 2.

7. Gammond, p. 46.

BiBLioGRAPHY

Reading List

Probably more has been written about the Beatles than any other band in musical history. Hundreds of books and thousands of articles cover every conceivable aspect of the Beatles from their personal lives, to their musical lives, to their impact on society. Thus, any reading list covering the Beatles must be selective. The books listed here are considered by the author to be among the most important and reliable works about the Fab Four.

Baird, Julia with Geoffrey Giuliano. *John Lennon, My Brother*. New York: Henry Holt, 1988.

Best, Pete and Patrick Doncaster. *Beatle! The Pete Best Story*. New York: Dell Publishing Co., 1985.

Catone, Marc A. *As I Write This Letter: An American Generation Remembers*. Ann Arbor, Mich.: Pierian Press, 1982.

Coleman, Ray. *Lennon: The Definitive Biography*. New York: HarperPerennial, 1992.

Davies, Hunter. *The Beatles: The Authorized Biography*. New York: McGraw-Hill, 1968.

Epstein, Brian. *A Cellarful of Noise*. New York: Doubleday, 1964.

Fast, Julius. *The Beatles: The Real Story*. New York: G. P. Putnam's Sons, 1968.

Giuliano, Geoffrey. *Blackbird: The Life and Times of Paul McCartney*. New York: Dutton, 1991.

Giuliano, Geoffrey. *Dark Horse: The Secret Life of George Harrison*. New York: Dutton, 1990.

Harrison, George. *I, Me, Mine*. New York: Simon and Schuster, 1980.

Harry, Bill, ed. *Mersey Beat: The Beginnings of the Beatles*. London, New York: Omnibus Press, 1977.

Harry, Bill. *The Ultimate Beatles Encyclopedia*. New York: Hyperion, 1992.

Hertsgaard, Mark. *A Day in the Life: The Music and Artistry of the Beatles*. New York: Delacorte Press, 1995.

Lennon, Cynthia. *A Twist of Lennon*. New York: Avon, 1980.

Lennon, John. *In His Own Write*. New York: Simon and Schuster, 1964.

Lennon, John. *A Spaniard in the Works*. New York: Simon and Schuster, 1965.

Lewisohn, Mark. *The Beatles Live!* New York: Henry Holt, 1986.

Lewisohn, Mark. *The Beatles Recording Sessions*. New York: Crown Publishers, 1988.

Lewisohn, Mark. *The Complete Beatles Chronicles*. New York: Harmony Books, 1992.

McCabe, Peter and Robert D. Schonfeld. *Apple to the Core*. New York: Pocket Books, 1972.

McDonald, Ian. *Revolution in the Head: The Beatles Records and the Sixties*. New York: Henry Holt, 1994.

McKeen, William. *The Beatles: A Bio-Bibliography*. Westport, Conn.: Greenwood Press, 1989.

Martin, George. *All You Need Is Ears*. New York: St. Martin's Press, 1980.

Mellers, Wilfrid. *Twilight of the Gods: The Beatles in Retrospect*. New York: Viking Press, 1974.

Norman, Philip. *Shout! The Beatles in Their Generation*. New York: Simon and Schuster, 1981.

O'Grady, Terence J. *The Beatles: A Musical Evolution*. Boston: Twayne, 1983.

Pang, May and Henry Edwards. *Loving John: The Untold Story*. New York: Warner Books, 1983.

Pawlowski, Gareth L. *How They Became the Beatles*. New York: E. P. Dutton, 1989.

Schultheiss, Tom, ed. *A Day in the Life: The Beatles Day-by-Day*. Ann Arbor, Mich.: Pierian Press, 1980.

Weiner, Jon. *Come Together: John Lennon in His Time*. New York: Random House, 1984.

Films and Videos

Films featuring the Beatles (most available on videocassette):
A Hard Day's Night. United Artists, 1964.
Help! United Artists, 1965.
Magical Mystery Tour. Apple Films, 1967.
Yellow Submarine (animation). United Artists, 1968.
Let it Be. United Artists, 1970.

Films about the Beatles:
Backbeat. Polygram Filmed Entertainment and Scala Productions, 1993 (film and videocassette).
The Beatles: The First U.S. Visit. Apple Corps Ltd., 1991 (videocassette).
The Compleat Beatles. Delilah Films, 1992 (videocassette).

Other Sources of Information

Center for Studies in Popular Culture, Bowling Green State University, Bowling Green, Ohio 43403. Probably the largest collection of Beatles materials in the United States.

The Rock and Roll Hall of Fame and Museum, One Key Plaza, Cleveland, Ohio 44114.

Beatlefan. P.O. Box 33515, Decatur, Georgia 30033. William P. King, publisher. A fan magazine published six times a year by the Goody Press.

Good Day Sunshine: The Beatles Fan Club. 397 Edgewood Avenue, New Haven, Connecticut 06511. Charles F. Rosenay!!!, president. Publication: *Good Day Sunshine.*

Beatlefest. P.O. Box 436, Westwood, New Jersey 07675-0436. Holds Beatles conventions several times a year in major cities. Publishes catalog of Beatles merchandise. Mark and Carol Lapidos.

Internet information: Usenet Newsgroup Rec.Music. Beatles.

DISCOGRAPHY: THE BEATLES ON RECORD

The listing of Beatles recordings presented here are all United States releases, and most are still available in record stores. Early on the Beatles had little control over their U.S. albums and record companies took liberties in altering the original titles and content of English versions. The assumption was that the same product would not appeal to both British and American audiences. It was apparently a faulty conclusion, based on what happened later. From *Sgt. Pepper* on releases were largely uniform worldwide with no apparent loss in sales. The selective list that follows is arranged chronologically. All are Capitol releases unless otherwise noted.

1962—Single: "My Bonnie" / "The Saints" (Decca).
1963—Album: *Introducing the Beatles* (Vee Jay).
        Singles: "Please Please Me" / "Ask Me Why" (Vee Jay); "From Me to You" / "Thank You Girl"(Vee Jay); "She Loves You" \ "I'll Get You" (Swan); "I Want to Hold Your Hand" / "I Saw Her Standing There."

1964—Albums: *Meet the Beatles; The Beatles Second Album; A Hard Day's Night; Something New; Beatles '65.*
Singles: "Can't Buy Me Love" / "You Can't Do That"; "A Hard Day's Night" / "I Should Have Known Better"; "I'll Cry Instead" / "I'm Just Happy to Dance with You"; "And I Love Her" / "If I Fell"; "I Feel Fine" / "She's a Women."

1965—Albums: *The Early Beatles; Help!; Rubber Soul.*
Singles: "Eight Days a Week" / "I Don't Want to Spoil the Party"; "Ticket to Ride" / "Yes It Is"; "Help!" / "I'm Down"; "Yesterday" / "Act Naturally"; "We Can Work It Out" / "Day Tripper."

1966—Albums: *Yesterday and Today; Revolver.*
Singles: "Nowhere Man" / "What Goes On"; "Paperback Writer" / "Rain"; "Yellow Submarine" / "Eleanor Rigby."

1967—Albums: *Sgt. Pepper's Lonely Hearts Club Band; Magical Mystery Tour.*
Singles: "Strawberry Fields Forever" / "Penny Lane"; "All You Need Is Love" / "Baby You're a Rich Man"; "Hello Goodbye"/ "I Am the Walrus."

1968—Album: *The Beatles* (The White Album).
Singles: "Lady Madonna" / "The Inner Light"; "Hey Jude" / "Revolution" (Apple).

1969—Albums: *Yellow Submarine* (Apple); *Abbey Road* (Apple; Capitol).
Singles: "Get Back" / "Don't Let Me Down" (Apple); "The Ballad of John and Yoko" (features only John and Paul) / "Old Brown Shoe" (Apple); "Something" / "Come Together" (Apple).

1970—Albums: *Let It Be* (Apple; Capitol); *Hey Jude* (Apple; Capitol).
Single: "Let It Be" / "You Know My Name."

1973—Albums: *The Beatles 1962–1966* (Apple; Capitol); *The Beatles 1967–1970* (Apple; Capitol).

1976—Album: *Rock 'n' Roll Music.*

1977—Albums: *The Beatles Live at the Hollywood Bowl;*

1977— *(continued from page 203)*
    The Beatles Live! At the Star Club in Hamburg Germany:
    1962 (Lingasong/Atlantic); *Love Songs.*
1980—Album: *The Beatles Rarities.*
1982—Album: *Reel Music.*
1983—Album: *The Beatles 20 Greatest Hits.*
1988—Album: *Past Masters, volumes I and II.*
1994—Album: *Live At The BBC* (Apple; Capitol).
1995—Albums: *The Beatles Anthology I* (Apple; Capitol).
1996—Album: *The Beatles Anthology II* (Apple; Capitol).

iNDEX

ABOUT THE AUTHOR

Marvin Martin is a freelance writer who often writes on educational subjects, including music. He is a board member and publications editor of the Rochelle Lee Fund, a nonprofit educational institution. A former advertising copy writer and encyclopedia editor, he is the father of four children. Mr. Martin lives in Chicago.

3/06   2   8/02

J
92
M

Martin, Marvin.

The Beatles.

DATE			

5/09		7		1/08
7-16		9		2-12
4/17	9			—
7/19		11		10/18
2/22		11		10/18

BAKER & TAYLOR